SELF-DISCOVERY

THROUGH THE

TAROT

THE
INNER FLAME
METHOD

CLAUDIA GENEST

FINDHORN
Press

First Published by Findhorn Press 2003

ISBN 1 84409 021 3

British Library Cataloguing-in-Publication Data.
A catalogue record for this book is available from
the British Library.

Edited by Lynn Barton
Cover design by Damien Keenan
Back cover design by Thierry Bogliolo
Internal book design by Karin Bogliolo

Printed and bound by WS Bookwell, Finland
Published by
Findhorn Press
305a The Park, Findhorn
Forres IV36 3TE
Scotland, UK
tel 01309 690582
fax 01309 690036
email: info@findhornpress.com
findhornpress.com

TABLE OF CONTENTS

	Introduction	7
1.	**Self-Discovery Through the Tarot**	9
	Building a Relationship to your Hieroglyphs through Meditation	13
2	**Brief History of the Tarot**	16
	My Quest for Tarot's Roots	19
3	**Spiritual Hieroglyphs:**	
	The Court Cards of the Minor Arcana	23
	Finding Your Spiritual Hieroglyph	25
	Meditation Exercise on your Spiritual Hieroglyph	27
4	**The Personality, Life, Lesson,**	
	and Hidden Hieroglyphs	29
	The Major Arcana 0-21	29
	Your Personality, Life, Lesson and Hidden Hieroglyphs:	32

5	**Understanding the Spiritual Hieroglyphs**	**40**
	The Tarot Tools And Their associated Star Signs	40
	Fire Star Signs	43
	Water Star Signs	45
	Air Star Signs	48
	Earth Star Signs (feminine principle)	51
	Interpretations of Spiritual Hieroglyphs	52
6	**Interpretations of the Personality, Life and Lesson Hieroglyphs: Major Arcana cards 0–21**	**78**
7	**The Guidance Hieroglyphs** **Ace – 10 of the Minor Arcana**	**118**
	Introduction to the Guidance Hieroglyphs	118
	How to Use The Guidance Hieroglyphs	121
	Interpretations of the Guidance Hieroglyphs	127
	Summary	**137**
	Suggested Reading	**138**
	Example of Life Lesson Diagram	**140**

Dedication

This book is written in honour of the Egyptian ancestors of Tarot. It is written with the spirit of cabala at its heart, with gratitude to the runes for their Nordic knowledge, to numerology for its power, and to astrology for its cosmic energy of stars, planets, and the universe. Gratitude is also extended to Native peoples world-wide for their Mother Earth wisdom, to the Stone people who give us treading spaces, to mythology for its stories, to the forever moving modern day, and in honour of all those who have crossed our paths.

Statement

The story of Tarot's creation may have begun in the ancient temples of Egypt. The mysteries of Tarot's true origins remain unsolved, while the teachings of the 'mirror of man' are with us to this day.

ACKNOWLEDGEMENTS

Kind words seem insufficient as I write this. First of all, thanks to my parents for giving me my breath and breathing spaces. My appreciation goes to Norbert Korte who gave me the incentive to learn and integrate the Tarot into my life. Thank you also to Kay Cordell Whitaker, Victor Wishalla and Lee Parisot for being the ones who seeded the moment of accepting, so I may express the knowledge that resides in me to the rest of the world. I extend my deepest thanks to Séamas O'Daimhín, my proof-reader, who stood at my side relentlessly without tiring. Thank you to the ladies at the Elgin Library who gave me space to write and showed incredible customer service skills. My appreciation is extended to Lynn Barton my editor, who patiently stuck to the job at hand. My deepest gratitude goes to my pal, Allan Robertson, a 'knight in shining armour' who came in the most unexpected moments to support me. There are so many more who have helped – I appreciate all of you.

Introduction

Are you missing the fire that resides in you? Does your spiritual purpose burn bright throughout each and very day, or is it a flicker so small you hardly know it is there? Are you connected to the true you, or to an image derived from other people's perceptions and comments?

Take some time right now to breathe deeply into your body, into your very core. Connect for a moment with you. This is your time. It is no accident that you have this book in your hands, it is a response to a call from within, a desire to learn about your spiritual purpose through the Inner Flame method and to reclaim what is missing. Welcome to your journey of self-discovery with the Tarot.

Mention Tarot cards to most people and they immediately think of divination, or fortune telling, with cards laid out in various ways to answer questions. I ask you to drop all such preconceptions. The interpretations in this book are designed for self-exploration and insight and not for use in divination in any way – they are far more powerful than that.

I feel it is time to demystify the Tarot and show just how much it can help with your personal development and spiritual growth. I encourage you to experiment with my suggestions as I introduce you to this process. Instead of approaching the Tarot with your mind, take this opportunity to allow all your senses to partake.

This guide introduces you to Tarot as a method for self-discovery. It will show you what elements you can rekindle. It will show hidden aspects, parts of yourself that are quietly living within your spiritual being, just waiting to come to the surface. Now is the time to let the cards weave themselves into your life and to choose to leave behind whatever is weighing you down. Allow the Tarot to help you gain the confidence to recognise and throw out all that no longer serves you on your life journey. This is your chance for a new beginning.

You have chosen to find another piece in the puzzle of your life that is residing deep inside you – the piece you maybe felt was lost – and to ignite the essence of your spiritual being. The Inner Flame method will gently assist you through joys and sorrows. This is a very personal journey. Let it teach you not to cling on to life as it is – no more 'making do'. Using the Inner Flame method will shine a new light on trials and tribulations, past and present, reframing them as lessons, signposts, or stepping-stones along your path.

In order to understand your spiritual purpose in life, it is essential to reclaim your self-confidence. Take time while reading to learn where your power lies, and to find your inner equilibrium. The Inner Flame method will give you confidence to seek, make, and accept changes within your own universe. I welcome you to this new and exciting approach to Tarot – as an agent of change – one that will enable you to broaden your horizons.

The Inner Flame method shows you what to do in order to make changes. You may be afraid of change, and yet one of the most beautiful things about being human is that you truly are never the same – physically, mentally, or emotionally. With every breath you take your cells change, your skin dies and replaces itself, your body is in a constant process of change. Each action you take impacts on your surroundings and offers you an experience, presenting you with options about what to do next. You allow yourself to learn and grow mentally and emotionally. As you walk through life your wishes, dreams and aspirations are fuelled by a desire to change, so that you can progress and feel whole.

I have spent many years with countless people developing the art of self-discovery using Tarot cards and I invite you to join me while I share my particular experience with you. This book will tell you how my ideas developed while including some history and basic information about the Tarot. It will also provide you with interpretations of the cards, empowering you to use the cards in your own individual way. As you take your steps, the Inner Flame method will support you in the rekindling of your own inner flame.

Chapter 1

SELF-DISCOVERY THROUGH THE TAROT

In order to begin with the Inner Flame method you will need your birth date and birth time (don't worry if you do not know your birth time, it is possible to continue without it, as I will explain later) and a deck of Tarot cards. Using the date and time of your birth you can choose your particular cards, apply the interpretations to your life and discover the lessons you could take in order to develop and progress spiritually. This method is designed to enable you to remain harmonious with your spiritual purpose.

Any Tarot deck enables you to dip into the deeper meaning of your life, so it is not necessary for you to work with a particular deck in order to use the Inner Flame method. However, it is preferable to use a deck which has images on the Guidance hieroglyph cards (Ace – 10 cards of the Minor Arcana), but if you have come to cherish your deck and it has only the number of the tool and a keyword such as Strength (9 of Rods), you may work with the cards in the best way available to you. You could for example paint an image, or meditate on the interpretations in this book in order to get a sense of what the Guidance hieroglyph is teaching you.

Use your deck without reference to the book that originally accompanied it. Many Tarot books include upside-down interpretations. All hieroglyphs in this book are interpreted right side up, as it is not part of the Inner Flame method to interpret them any other way.

Tarot cards speak a language all of their own. The cards are the results of ancient insights depicted in symbols, and these symbols offer a framework to help you see more clearly. The cards represent the quintessence of all that exists in the human spirit in its purest form. Tarot speaks of getting to know all aspects of the self – including the imagination, the feelings, the intellect, and the instincts.

Using the Tarot as a learning method creates a space in which you can explore and access your willingness to make personal choices with no outside influence. The Inner Flame method offers you the chance to become congruent and be guided by your intuition. With this method you can pick up and begin to follow a thread that you may have lost, and begin to weave new elements into your life. The cards leave an imprint on your mind, while they also go a lot deeper.

Throughout the book, I have referred to all the main card groups as hieroglyphs. The word hieroglyph – which means holy writings – is used to create a connection to the ancient Egyptian roots of Tarot, which seemed appropriate for a book based on reconnecting you to the roots of your spiritual being. It is also used to give you a sense of the holiness within you.

The ancient Egyptians believed that true learning comes from personal experience, not from others. It can be all too easy to cling to the words of teachers, scholars and masters who profess to know the truth, but I encourage you to remember: teachers can only show you a way of learning, the greatest lessons come from personal experience. The Tarot used with the Inner Flame Method becomes a tool for that experience, it hands the power back to you – where it belongs.

Your hieroglyphs can be helpers or silent observers to accompany you along in life; they are at your disposal as either subtle or obvious companions. What you do with them, how you apply them, and how you use them is entirely up to you.

A Tarot deck has 78 cards, which are traditionally divided into two sections:
- the Major Arcana (22 cards)
- and the Minor Arcana (56 cards)

To my surprise, I was unable to find a numerological definition for the number 78. The two closest numbers for which I could find a definition are 77 and 80:

    77 = repentance or forgiveness

    80 = restoration to health

Maybe 78 has been left undefined because it opens our perceptions to the things we did not see in the first instance. It is the number that leaves it up to us to discover its meaning. Could it be that after *forgiveness* comes *self-discovery* (through the 78 cards of the Tarot), which leads to a *restoration of health* on all levels?

These are the types of hieroglyphs we will be exploring with:

• **Spiritual Hieroglyphs** – derived from the 16 court cards of the Minor Arcana

• **Personality and Life Hieroglyphs** – derived from the 22 cards of the Major Arcana (can be one or two cards, depending on your date and time of birth).

• **Lesson Hieroglyphs** – derived from the 22 cards of the Major Arcana. These are cards that accompany you in particular years.

• **Guidance Hieroglyphs** – derived from the 40, Ace to 10 cards of the Minor Arcana.

• **Hidden Hieroglyphs** – derived from the 22 Major Arcana cards. The hidden hieroglyph is exactly what it says. Its influence quietly stays in the background and does not obviously surface. They are re-minders, gently nudging you to make changes.

Be gentle with yourself. As I introduce you to Tarot as a tool for change, it may become difficult at times for you to get a sense of what you can do in order to understand your Spiritual, Personality, Life, Lesson and Hidden Hieroglyphs. You may feel impatient and want to skip a section or two. I suggest that you take your time and be patient. Trust that all you need will come to you. You are about to transform your life – this is not something to hurry.

Later in the book, as you read the interpretations of the hieroglyphs, you may find elements in some of them with which you resonate, even though they are not your own. I recommend that you focus on your own particular hieroglyphs. If the interpretations of other hieroglyphs make you think, "That's me!" then I recommend you work with them as Hidden hieroglyphs (see later section).

Remember, your own particular hieroglyphs represent the key to understanding yourself. They are your first priority. Identifying with them will assist you to nourish your spiritual essence. Allow them to help you reclaim the strength and power to be you.

Connections between the hieroglyphs and various schools of thought, such as cabala, astrology, runes, numerology, mythology, etc. are made throughout the book. These references are designed to give you the incentive and inspiration to gain further knowledge from these schools of thought. They are only briefly touched upon, as deeper knowledge is outside the scope of this book.

The hieroglyphs can also function as a valuable addition to astrology readings, the runes, cabala, psychotherapies, and any other type of assistive methods. Tarot hieroglyphs work by showing you another angle. The cards speak to you in a pictorial form. The symbols on the cards can also infuse new feelings and leave a lasting impression on your subconscious mind.

The tools (rods, cups, swords and pentacles) on the cards play a major role when learning to connect to your spiritual purpose with the Inner Flame method. They influence your approach to life significantly. For example, if a rod is on the card, it means that your first impulse will be to react with fire energy. You will find an in-depth description of each tool's form of expression later in the book.

Over the years, many scholars have studied the word Tarot and what lies hidden among its letters. The study of the formation of words and the letters used dates back to ancient times, when words were first invented. Much has been written about the power of words and deciphering the messages that often lie within them. I do not have the space here to go into this in depth – but you may like to try it with your own name.

Here are some of the ancient words found hidden within T-a-r-o-t:

- T-o-r-a(h) (meaning 'law of evolution')
- T-r-o-a (a 'gate')
- R-a-t-o ('realisation')
- R-o-t-a ('evolving wheel of life')
- O-r-a-t ('request')
- A-t-o-r ('God of initiation').
- O-t-a-r ('listening')
- A-r-o-t ('the work')
- T-a-r ('way' or 'path')
- R-o ('royal')
- T-a-u-r-t ('the Goddess responsible for fertility and protection of the feminine', written in Egyptian mythology as Thoueris)
- T-a-r-o ('destiny')

Building a Relationship to your Hieroglyphs through Meditation

In one form or another meditation has been practiced by every culture and religion on earth. In our modern world, it is not always easy to find some quiet amid the chaos, but through meditation each and every one of us can reconnect with our true and peaceful nature. Meditation allows you to still the mind and find contemplation and completion within. It helps you to understand yourself more deeply. Meditation is an excellent way to build a relationship with your hieroglyphs.

If you are attempting meditation for the first time, I suggest you spend some time to gather information about the many different types of meditation. Attending a meditation group and/or a workshop is a great way to learn the basics of whichever meditation practice you choose. However, may people meditate very happily alone with no guidance or tuition from anyone.

A technique to get you started:

Find a time when you are least likely to be interrupted – maybe turn the phone off and put a 'do not disturb' sign on your door. Wear loose comfortable clothing and make sure the room is warm enough, without being over heated. Give yourself about half an hour to start with.

Sit in a comfortable upright position – either on the floor or on a straight-backed chair (crossed legs are not obligatory). Take a while to make sure you are comfortable; maybe use cushions to support your lower back if you feel yourself slouching. Allow your body to relax and take a few full deep breaths, becoming aware of any areas where you feel tension and letting it go with each out breath.

As you begin to feel comfortable and quiet, focus on your breathing, following the breath in and out…in and out. There is no need to change the quality or pace of the breath, just follow its rhythm. Your mind WILL wander – it's what minds do –when this happens just gently bring it back to your breath.

Once you are comfortable with whichever type of meditation you choose, you can start to visualize your hieroglyphs during meditation. Hold the images in your mind's eye and see what happens. If you are not a visual person, you could maybe try contemplating the meaning of the cards instead.

When building a relationship to your hieroglyphs, meditating with them assists you in connecting with your roots. The pictures on the cards are expressions of you from birth, and of the tasks you have faced in the past, those in the present, and those likely to occur in the future. Meditating also facilitates identification with the character on the cards, making it easier for you to accept and understand yourself. You will also find yourself developing your own thoughts and allowing new ideas to come forward. This can be particularly useful when you are confronted with challenges.

Through meditation, you are taking responsibility for your wellbeing, while the hieroglyphs act as anchoring agents. This is how you can connect to your self-belief and power to change. You may begin getting insights about yourself you never had before. Respect these insights and give yourself time for this kind of inner work.

I have also made reference to other sources of study in this book because the Inner Flame method can take many directions. Taking this into account, I suggest that you start meditating, studying, and exchanging your thoughts with others at some point in time. Many find it useful to form a group who can meet, meditate, and study together.

Chapter 2

BRIEF HISTORY OF THE TAROT

To this day, scholars of the Tarot are still puzzled about its *actual* origins. One of the most popular theories and the one most widely studied is the possibility that it was born in Egypt. This theory certainly appeals the most to me. For instance, the Tarot has been connected to Thoth, the Lord of Wisdom, who was depicted with the head of an ibis. He was the Neter (similar to a god or deity) of reckoning, learning, time, writing, and of the moon. Thoth symbolized masculine energy. He was revered in the period between 664–522 B.C when his cult centred in the town of Khmunu in Upper Egypt. He shared his responsibility for writing and inventing hieroglyphs with the Neter Seshat, who brought balance with her female energy, keeping records and organising his writings.

Thoth's teachings can be studied in the *Book of Thoth*, a book designed to make people think about their world, about existence and spirituality. And with enigmatic statements like the following, you can see how it probably did just that:

There is one single truth and there is no single truth

(from *the Book of Thoth*)

From the time of the ancient Egyptians up to the fourteenth century, not much was recorded about the Tarot. It is believed the Tarot was first brought to Europe between 1370 and 1420. During this time, gypsies (the name is derived from the words E-g-y-p-t-i-a-n-s) are said to have begun using Tarot cards to tell fortunes, which is something that has continued into modern day.

Tarocchi, (the oldest surviving cards) appeared in Italy in the fifteenth century. They were hand painted, so the images on them were originals, although at that time scholars believed the pictures had been copied from other sources.

Antoine Court de Gebelin (1725–1787), a Mason and pastor, was a well-known researcher of the Tarot during his lifetime. He was fond of Egyptian mythology and created a theory around the card's origin in a lengthy nine-volume work called Le Monde Primitif, written about 1200 years after the Egyptians had used hieroglyphs. This work, which became quite popular in its time, was aimed at convincing scholars of the Tarot's connection to the ancient Egyptian schools. He theorised that the depictions on the cards were used as tools of initiation into Egyptian priesthood.

In Gebelin's opinion, the Major Arcana was the pictorial form of the teachings in the Book of Thoth. He believed the priests rescued these hieroglyphs from the temples and libraries before the buildings were burnt – either by accident or intention in the restless times of invasion and uprising. He wrote that the priests, in fear of losing their knowledge, deliberately hid the scriptures in order to ensure it would survive Christianity and the collapse of paganism. He was also convinced that magical knowledge lay hidden in the cards.

In the time after Gebelin's work was published, religious authorities – specifically Christian clergymen – felt threatened by the growing interest in ancient knowledge and began a campaign to suppress the Tarot. As a result of their actions, scholars of the Tarot did not publish many books during this period, although some did secretly continue their studies.

In the nineteenth and twentieth centuries the Tarot eventually became more accepted and scholars were once again free to continue their probing into its uses and origins. The first author to gain recognition was Eliphas Levi (approximately 1810–1850), a priest and Rosicrucian. He introduced the public to his theory of a connection between the Tarot and the mystical Jewish teachings of the Cabala (meaning 'tradition' in Hebrew).

Levi also connected the cards to scriptures in the Bible and other ancient spiritual writings, including the Book of Thoth. He was also notably the first to link the Major Arcana to the letters of the Hebrew alphabet and the letters he applied to the 22 cards still apply today. Some readers may want to study the cabala in addition to the Tarot in order to widen their knowledge, and may also like to read more about Levi's links to the Hebrew alphabet – a subject which exceeds the scope of this book.

The next interesting author was another Mason, Paul Christian (born 1863), who believed the images on the cards were derived from those painted in the temples, palaces, and homes of ancient Egypt. Additionally, Papus (1865–1916), a doctor and philosopher, claimed the images were painted onto pyramid walls in Egypt for initiation purposes and also believed they were inscribed in the secret chambers of Egyptian temples. Today, Egyptologists are researching these inscriptions and their purpose.

In 1888, Samuel Liddell 'MacGregor' Mathers (1854–1918), co-founded the Order of the Golden Dawn – a school for students of old, or occult knowledge, in London – with William Wynn Westcott (1848–1925). The Order offered courses that included meditating on the Tarot cards, practising rituals, examining horoscopes, and studying ancient teachings.

Aleister Crowley, a member of the Golden Dawn Order (1875–1947), developed the Aleister Crowley Thoth Tarot deck with Lady Frieda Harris (1877–1962). Working with and teaching occult methods did not gain him much public recognition during his own lifetime, but his Tarot deck is widely used today. I was particularly fascinated to see that Crowley pointed out how important it is to identify with the cards as a means to self-discovery.

A.E. Waite, a Freemason (1857–1947), made a significant contribution to the Tarot along with artist, Pamela Coleman-Smith (1878–1951). Together they produced one of today's popular decks, the Universal Rider-Waite Tarot.

Everyone who has studied the Tarot since its inception has made valuable contributions to the Tarot as we know it today – to its use, history, and the interpretations of the cards. The books, the theories of the Tarot's origins and the card decks are endless and diverse. It can be a delight to study the many historically based works, as well as decks such as the Haindl Tarot, White Eagle Medicine Wheel Tarot, and Morgan-Greer Tarot. If you feel motivated to look into the history of the Tarot in more depth, check out the suggested reading list at the back of the book.

My Quest for Tarot's Roots

The fascination regarding the Tarot lies in the very mystery of its roots. The question of where the cards come from cannot be answered with great certainty and seeking their origin and purpose becomes a quest for many – as it was for myself.

My studies began in 1984, when I began investigating the old books about the Tarot in the Deutsche Bibliotheca (Frankfurt, Germany), in old bookshops in Paris, France, and at the British Library in London. As a result, the many other schools – such as astrology, the cabala, and numerology – that touched the Tarot also began to interest me.

The old books tossed and turned me through a maze of times past. I became engrossed in worlds I had never imagined existed. It became important to me to study structures of ancient societies and to forage into the various forms of learning that ancient peoples accepted as part of their lives.

Of all the books I studied, those connecting to the Egyptian past of the Tarot caught my attention the most. I was fascinated to learn how much divination was part of that ancient world, how Egyptian priests tossed their sticks upon the altars in the chambers of the temples to help make their personal decisions, and how this same approach even played a role in the governmental decision-making.

Meeting an amazing man called Norbert Korte, in 1984, inspired my own studies. It was he who introduced me to the Tarot cards and his approach to using them for one's own learning and self-discovery. He also applied the cards to group work in order to intensify the experience of their teachings.

When the cards were laid out in front of me for the first time, I was overwhelmed by their effect upon me. I felt like I was being initiated, and also had a sense of connection to an ancient source that I could not explain. Norbert taught me how to find my own cards and how to work with them as channels to develop and grow spiritual strengths that reside within me. Exploring the cards in this way led me to developing new ways to work with them – and it led to the writing of this book.

As I began to work with the cards as a tool for self-discovery, my general awareness sharpened profoundly. Suddenly the characters and symbols of the Tarot began appearing to me in different places around the world. I saw them in homes, on church windows or portals, sitting on shrines, decorating buildings, in hospitals, and worn as charms by people on the street. I was being initiated into seeing the world with different eyes. For me, the Tarot became a depiction of the human spirit in all its forms and expressions.

It seemed that the more knowledge I gained, the more I wanted to find out, so I travelled further and wider in my quest to find Tarot's roots and to further understand its many uses.

During one of my journeys, I went to Egypt, the land of Thoth. I felt if I placed myself in this ancient world, whose people were custodians of a long lost culture, it might help me to understand more. I went with no fixed plans and instead followed my instincts. My intuition led me to visit the Temples of Isis, Karnak, Luxor, the Great Pyramids, and the Egyptian Museum in Cairo. I felt myself drawn by the fascination of the ancient images.

I took time to listen to the sounds of the temples and to study the old structures. I meditated, spoke to guides, and created a connection to the buildings and the land with my senses. I studied the hieroglyphs in the temples and reflected on their imagery – similarities to the characters in Tarot cards struck me deeply. My intrigue with this ancient connection matched that of Papus, Gebelin, Christian, and the others who had gone before me. I was never alone on my quest.

My personal belief in Tarot's connection to Egypt was greatly strengthened. However, there was one puzzle that remained unsolved: The temples were constructed between 2500 B.C. and 1200 B.C., yet scholars claimed the images of the Tarot were not developed until ca. 700 B.C. Though I left Egypt without answers to all my questions, I did leave full of new ideas and thoughts.

A few years later, I came across information about a place destroyed many, many years ago in Egypt: the Temple Beautiful. I was fascinated. It is believed this temple of healing, study, religious teachings, and arts is even older than the temples I had seen, dating back to a time before Thoth was worshipped. In ancient Egypt, the arts were seen as a channel to educate and transform societal structures and this was one of the temples erected to attract those willing to develop their inherent creativity. People could go there to be healed, or to become students, learning the essence of their spirit. At that time, the continuation of Egyptian society relied on having initiates who would learn for this purpose. It is said that their insights were needed to serve the future of the country.

In the Temple Beautiful, a variety of methods helped to strengthen the students' awareness of themselves. The teachers, or priests, had the ability to psychically link with the students. They used sound vibrations and different coloured flashing lights to initiate the students who entered the temple. Such practises affected the vibratory levels of the student's bodies and heightened their sensitivity. Dancing and chanting were common, helping them to become one with the music in order to purify the body and introduce them to the mystery of creation. This was how initiates transcended into the creative forces of deeper awareness.

What intrigued me most was the thought that Tarot cards could have been developed in this most ancient of Temples. I wondered if the students were maybe asked to work with the Tarot images, allowing the priests to then experiment with the knowledge gained. As a result of the political situation in the ancient world it is possible that the priests may have later encrypted the pictures in hieroglyphs for the purpose of safekeeping them.

The drawings may have been as popular then as they are today. The only difference might have been that only priests or initiates could use them. The old texts I studied reminded me again and again how they all adhered to strict codes of practice to keep certain knowledge as protected as possible.

I felt that the students saw deeply into their souls when they were initiated, much as my friends and myself did when working in this manner. They could have easily visualised the images that the Tarot of today depicts after experiencing themselves deeply. The priests may have then decided they could use the drawings to gain deeper insights.

This could mean that ancient Egyptians identified with the pictures in order to change their perception of their world. The cards have certainly done this for me. My practical experience with the Tarot cards has also confirmed that identification with the cards is a way of discovering deeper knowledge about my inner flame.

In any case, the priests must have been aware of how these pictures from their initiates depicted every internal psychological event and experience of life with amazing accuracy. Were they the ones who began to create the Tarot? Or were the Priests the ones who began using their initiate's drawings to teach deeper understanding? I am unable to answer these questions. As a result, my quest for Tarot's roots remains a lifelong journey.

Chapter 3

SPIRITUAL HIEROGLYPHS:
THE COURT CARDS OF THE Minor Arcana

All 16 court cards (four kings, queens, knights and pages) of the Minor
Arcana are spiritual hieroglyphs. They represent what I have defined as
the 16 spiritual archetypes. In numerological literature, 16 means love,
happiness, and integrity. Therefore, these cards as a whole can represent
the path to integrity.

Your spiritual hieroglyph is the first stepping-stone to your inner
flame, it describes your spiritual qualities and deepens your understanding of your basic spiritual needs, showing that you have a unique spiritual purpose in life that differentiates you from others. It also depicts
the essential way you thrive in the world and the 'tool' (rod, cup, sword
or pentacle) you apply to align with your own energy.

Card	Basic action
king	"I observe"
queen	"I decide"
knight	"I act"
page	"I experience"

In nature, the spiritual hieroglyph can be seen as the seed of a plant,
containing the essence of growth. The tools would represent the seed's
ability to grow. Another metaphor would be the building of a house.
Imagine the essence of growth is to decide to build a house (represented
by the king, queen, knight or page in the deck), and how you go about
building the house is decided through the tool (rod, cup, sword, or
pentacle) you use – so the tool is how the plan unfolds.

Which way your character faces

• Looking left

When a court character has his or her head turned to the left, the character instinctively bases his or her observations, feelings, thoughts, or manifestations on the past. This means that when you have a hieroglyph with a character looking to the left you instinctively act, feel, think or manifest with your subconscious mind, you may be introverted, and investigate inner worlds and dreams. You also see what happened in the past and regard that as important.

• Looking right

When the court character's head is to the right, that character's observations, feelings, thoughts, or manifestations are instinctively based on the future. This means that when you have a hieroglyph with a character looking to the right your spirit has evolved through external experiences. You instinctively bring along consciousness and are extroverted or involved in activity that has the future in mind.

• Looking ahead

When the court character is looking directly out of the card, it means his or her feelings, actions, feelings, thoughts, or actions are based on the present moment. This means that when you have a hieroglyph with a character looking ahead you are instinctively in the here and now. This means your form of expression can vary tremendously as you have a natural ability to empathise with any form of consciousness.

Please take note that different Tarot decks have the court character's heads facing in different directions. In this book, I have noted the main emphasis of your hieroglyph by saying that you are acting, feeling, thinking, or manifesting in the past, present, or future.

Studying the spiritual hieroglyphs reminds us of the many variations in people's characters – making it easier for us to understand others. Studying your friend's/partner's/work-colleague's spiritual hieroglyph can enhance your relationship by deepening your understanding and seeing how you can best relate to each other.

My goal is to encourage and enable you to make your own interpretations. For that reason the interpretations of the hieroglyphs that follow later are only meant to serve as illustrations, or examples. I encourage you to use meditation with the cards as a way to find your own truths.

Finding Your Spiritual Hieroglyph

Step 1: Finding Your Tool

Look for your star sign in the following list and discover the tool (rod, cup, sword, or pentacle) by which you are guided. Your inner patterns are ruled by the element (fire, water, air, or earth) of your tool, which shows the foundation of your actions.

Tools	Star Signs
Rods (fire: creative ideas)	Aries, Leo, Sagittarius
Cups (water: feelings)	Scorpio, Cancer, Pisces
Swords (air: thoughts)	Aquarius, Gemini, Libra
Pentacles (earth: manifestation or action)	Taurus, Capricorn, Virgo

Step 2: Finding Your Court Character

Take your ascendant star sign, which is calculated on the basis of your birth time and birthplace. If you do not already know your ascendant, then you can either ask an astrologer for your astrological chart, or go onto the Internet and search for websites that can calculate your ascendant for you. Next, look for your ascendant in the following list and discover the court character (king, queen, knight, or page) that represents you.

Court Character	Ascendant
King (fire element)	Aries, Leo, Sagittarius
Queen (water element)	Scorpio, Cancer, Pisces
Knight (air element)	Aquarius, Gemini, Libra
Page (earth element)	Taurus, Capricorn, Virgo

Step 3: Combining

Your spiritual hieroglyph is a combination of your tool and your court character. For example:

• if your star sign is Sagittarius (rods)
  and your ascendant is Gemini (knight),
  your spiritual hieroglyph is the Knight of Rods
• if your star sign is Pisces (cups)
  and your ascendant is Capricorn (page),
  your spiritual hieroglyph is the Page of Cups

You may like to write down the name of your own spiritual hieroglyph, or take that card from your deck and keep it with you as you work your way through the rest of this book.

Suggestions For Those Who Do Not Know Their Birth Time

If you have not been able to discover your birth time via a birth certificate or a relative try the following:

• *Ask a professional hypnotist, or psychic, to take you on a journey back to the time when you were born. The aim should be to enable you to visualise the time of day you were born.*

• *Look at the four court cards in your series (if you are a Sagittarian that would be the king, queen, knight and page of rods, for a Gemini it would be the king, queen, knight and page of swords...and so on) and see if one of them attracts your attention. You may feel immediately drawn to one, or it may take a little time. Pay attention to your intuition. You may want to consult different decks in order to see a wider range of depictions.*

Here are some helpful questions you can ask during this process:

• *Is my main preoccupation in life to examine, observe, and recognise the world around me? (king)*

• *Do I always feel that I must or should make decisions in my life? (queen)*

• *Do I mainly take action in the world? (knight)*

• *Do I mainly go through experiences, reflect on them and then act accordingly? (page)*

Trust your intuition. Once you have decided which card is your spiritual hieroglyph, put it in a special place for a period of time. Should you get the impulse to change the card, then choose a new one (reflecting again on the questions above).

Meditation Exercise on your Spiritual Hieroglyph

• *Start by making yourself comfortable and taking a few deep breaths – releasing any tension in your body with each out breath.*

• *You are going on an inner journey. Spend a moment looking at your spiritual hieroglyph. You can either hold the card, put it on your lap, or place it in front of you as you meditate*

• *Close your eyes and take some more deep breaths. Wind your mind down and relax. This is your time. Take your attention to each part of your body, starting with your feet and working up towards your head. Send warm relaxing waves through each part of your body and let all tension simply melt away.*

• *Imagine you are the character on your spiritual hieroglyph. Become that person. Imagine you are wearing their clothes, holding their tool, and in the scene on the card. Are you standing or sitting? How does it feel to wear that outfit? Spend a while becoming familiar with your new character.*

• *Now imagine you are moving – maybe walking, or roaming. Where are you? Take note of all that is around you, the sights, smells, feelings, and sounds. Take some time and be the character, do whatever you want.*

• *Allow your story to unfold in your imagination. Enter fully into the experience.*

• *When you are ready, bid farewell to whoever you have met. Bring your attention back to your breathing and feel your own physical body again. Wriggle your fingers and toes and take your time to bring your attention back into the room. Open your eyes slowly and enjoy a stretch.*

• *Write your experience down. Begin a journal, which can become a useful reference book in the future. If you have dreams that appear to be significant (particularly following soon after a meditation) then you can also write them down.*

This exercise is just a way to get you started. In time, you will become your own expert in the best ways to learn from your hieroglyphs.

Chapter 4

THE PERSONALITY, LIFE, LESSON, AND HIDDEN HIEROGLYPHS

The Major Arcana 0–21

In Tarot literature, I noted that the term Major Arcana was described as meaning "human race", which to me represents the basic idea of the 22 cards. Major Arcana cards are said to depict the powers and virtues of the human spirit. The pictures are a mnemonic and they can lead us to knowledge we may not be aware is influencing us. The cards show the influences around mundane events and material powers as things that are manifest in our world.

The Major Arcana can lead us from not knowing something into developing awareness about things we did not know before. Its role is to show that everyone inevitably learns this in one way or another during the course of their lifetime. It expresses in picture form our personalities and the essence of our experiences, so that the sequences and main themes of our lives become visible.

The Major Arcana is made up of 22 cards. The number 22 in numerology is the number of all material things, leadership and powerful forces, which indicates that each hieroglyph is accompanied by polarised energy. Each card includes powerful forces, which give us a sense of leadership essential to making things manifest to their fullest potential. All this implies that the knowledge we need for life can be found in the Tarot images. The cards enable something to flow and/or dissolve. They definitely give pictorial impressions that go deeper into the subconscious than spoken words alone.

Lets have a look at the more traditional meanings of the 22 cards:

Cards 0 and 21 are usually defined as interchangeable cards. These cards can be at the beginning or at the end of our life's cycle and personal path.

These two cards begin and end the cycle of the Major Arcana. Overall, they show how our life cycle is circular and our processes can begin and end over and over again. Card 0 (the Fool) shows innocence and it represents 'simple' paradise. Card 21 (the World) shows completion and it represents 'complete' paradise.

Card 0 (the Fool) "I am nothing"

Card 21(the World) "My desires are fulfilled"

Cards 1–10 are Inner Processes: These processes represent the law of polarity (such as high/low; masculine/feminine, etc.) This is a basic law in a world of duality, where we humans experience ourselves as representatives of one of each of these polarities. In the teachings of the Tarot, we experience each process in order to become capable of dealing with everyday life. Imagine that the Major Arcana is like a ladder – each card a rung – we climb to reach a higher form of consciousness in our soul.

Cards 1–4 (the Magician, the High Priestess, the Empress, the Emperor) refer to the knowledge we are gaining and the lessons that we are learning as individuals. They depict the four basic spiritual essences that rule within our souls:

Card 1 (the Magician) "I am"

Card 2 (the High Priestess) "I am thinking"

Card 3 (the Empress) "I am feeling"

Card 4 (the Emperor) "I prevail"

Cards 5–6 (the Hierophant and the Lovers) show the celestial or angelic realms that reside in our spirit:

Card 5 (the Hierophant) "I unite"

Card 6 (the Lovers) "I decide on an inner level"

Cards 7–9 (the Chariot, Justice, the Hermit) are the paths of individual and personal initiation:

Card 7 (The Chariot) " I am moving onwards"

Card 8 (Justice) "I balance myself"

Card 9 (the Hermit) "I am content with myself"

Card 10 (the Wheel of Life) is at the top of a pentagram – at the top of a new cycle. As a new cycle in our spiritual development begins, this card floats between inner and outer processes, so we experience it both internally and externally.

Card 10 (the Wheel of Life)"I am creating a balance"

Cards 11–21 are Outer Processes. These processes are triggered by an event or events that happen externally. Yet, the expression of the processes is experienced within ourselves. When these events happen, we learn to realise that each of us is part of the 'bigger' picture. These cards open doors, so that we really learn from our previous experiences.

Cards 11–14 (Strength, the Hanged Man, the Devil, Temperance) depict the challenges humanity must conquer:

Card 11 (Strength) "I tame my instincts within"

Card 12 (the Hanged Man) "I see the world upside down"

Card 13 (Death) "I transform"

Card 14 (Temperance) "I renew the mixture"

Card 15 represents the taming of 'evil' influences, which for us means that transformation is something we must confront:

Card 15 (the Devil) "I have too much of one and too little of another"

Cards 16–19 (the Tower, the Star, the Moon and the Sun) are the spiritual tasks humans can undertake, while utilising the energy that affects our spiritual process:

Card 16 (the Tower) "I release in order to renew myself"

Card 17 (the Star) "I set creativity free"

Card 18 (the Moon) "I look deeply into the soul"

Card 19 (the Sun) "I see the light"

Card 20 (Judgment) depicts a form of spiritual enlightenment that we can attain through the effect of our actions:

Card 20 (Judgment) "I open the door to reveal paradise"

Your Personality, Life, Lesson and Hidden Hieroglyphs:

The 22 cards of the Major Arcana are the personality, life, lesson, and hidden hieroglyphs. They play the role of giving content to your world. The purpose of the interpretations of the cards is to allow you to see the basics you brought along as the parts of your inner flame.

Personality Hieroglyph

The personality hieroglyph is the second stepping-stone to your inner flame. This hieroglyph is the layout of your personality, the way it came into this world. It is depicted on a Tarot card in its pure form. Your personality hieroglyph shows the way you live here on earth. It represents the foundation of what you think, feel, and experience within yourself.

Life Hieroglyph

The life hieroglyph is the third stepping-stone to your inner flame. This hieroglyph is the picture of how you experience events, emotions, or challenges within. It tells you how your mind, body, and spirit instinctively react in the first moment.

Lesson Hieroglyph

The lesson hieroglyph is the fourth stepping-stone to your inner flame. This is the hieroglyph that accompanies you during a particular year. The year begins on your birthday and ends on the day before your next birthday. However, some people feel the effects of the beginning of a new year some time before or after their birthday.

This hieroglyph depicts the lessons that you could learn during that year in order to be aligned to your spiritual purpose, and to nourish your inner flame. It explains the lessons that you could integrate into your life.

Focusing on the lesson hieroglyphs from past years can strengthen your connection to your inner flame and help you to evolve through deeper self-understanding.

A Life Lesson Diagram

This is a way to map events of the past and see the lesson hieroglyphs that were influencing you at that time. It is interesting to maybe see patterns emerging, or lessons revisited. It can also help you to understand why things happened in the way they did and to focus on the bigger picture, showing the processes you have been through in regards to your spiritual purpose.

Up the left hand vertical side of the graph you enter the numbers of the Major Arcana cards 1–21. Then along the bottom of your graph enter the years of your life, starting at the left with your year of birth, and then add all the years to date. Under each year, make a note of special events that occurred during that time.

Examples: births/deaths, moving home, change of school, major illness, accidents, marriage, divorce, and career change. Add whatever seems significant and important to you in your life.

Use the calculations that follow to find your lesson hieroglyphs/s for those years and enter them on your graph by colouring or marking the appropriate squares in whichever way you choose. Then read the interpretations of the cards in Chapter 6.

You can also map Lesson Hieroglyphs for the future. If, for instance you were planning to get married, or have a major career change, then you can find out which lesson hieroglyph will be accompanying you in that year of change.

See an example of life lesson diagram at the back of this book on page 140.

Hidden Hieroglyph

The hidden hieroglyph is the fifth stepping-stone to your inner flame. It is exactly what it says. Its influence stays quietly in the background and does not obviously surface. However, it is possible for you to uncover it. You can make it live its hidden energy, so that something can be given the chance to shift.

✒Note: Although some of the hidden hieroglyphs have been noted in certain sections of the interpretations, be aware that you may have other hidden hieroglyphs. You can read the interpretations of the Major Arcana cards and discover your own hidden hieroglyphs. This means, if you are reading about a personality, life, or lesson hieroglyph and you notice that you express some of its archetypal qualities, then it could be a hidden hieroglyph that you could use to shift your energy.

Important Notes:

Use the personality, life, lesson, and hidden hieroglyphs with the spiritual hieroglyph when you want to intensify your learning process. Once you have begun, this kind of work automatically shifts energy in its own subtle way. From the very moment you know which hieroglyphs are yours, you can trust that they are silently sitting at your side to help you on your journey to self-discovery.

If you are someone who uses the Tarot for readings, I would suggest you add the inner flame method in the following way: Before choosing the cards for a reading, take your own hieroglyphs out of the deck. Lay them out right side up and then do a reading with the remaining cards. Your hieroglyphs will then relay their power and energy into the reading.

In my experience, you can have much more powerful and mind-expanding readings by doing this. When using Tarot cards for readings, you are advised not to use the interpretations in this book, which are solely designed for interpreting the four types of hieroglyphs

Finding your Personality, Life, Lesson and Hidden Hieroglyphs

To find your personality, life, and lesson hieroglyph you add together the date, month, and year and reduce the number down to 21 or less.

• **The personality and life hieroglyph** is calculated adding your date of birth and the year you were born. So, for example, if you were born on 24 August 1962, you would add 24 + 8 + 1962.

• **The lesson hieroglyph** is calculated adding the day and month of your birth date to the particular year you wish to calculate. So, if you were born on 28 November 1963 and wanted to study the lessons learnt in the year 2003, you would add 28 + 11 + 2003.

Reducing the number to 21 or less.

Example:

Date of birth – 24 August 1962.

$$
\begin{array}{r}
24 \\
+\ 8 \\
+1962 \\
\hline
\end{array}
$$

1994 = 1+9+9+4 = **23** – which is greater then 21, so…

you would then reduce by adding 2+3 = **5** (The Hierophant)

This would be written 5/5

If your total is already 21 or less

For totals between 1 and 9

In general, if the final sum of your calculation adds up to 9 or below (see following example), this means you have one card as your personality and life, or lesson hieroglyph.

Example:

Date of birth – 28 November 1963

28
+   11
+ 1963

2002 = 2+0+0+2 = **4** (a single figure, so stays as it is)

This means that card 4 – (The Emperor) would be your Personality *and* Life hieroglyph.

This would be written 4/4.

For totals between 10 and 21

If your calculation adds up to a number with double digits (between 10 and 21), this means you have two different cards to study. The first (larger) number you calculate is your personality hieroglyph. The second (smaller) number you calculate is your life hieroglyph.

Example:

26 October 2003.

26
+   10
+ 2003

2039 = 2+0+3+9 = 14 (Temperance) – Personality Hieroglyph

You would then add 1 + 4 = **5** (The Hierophant) – Life Hieroglyph

This would be written 14/5.

The sum of 19 is the exception!

An exception to the rule is if you calculate the sum of 19. Then you have three hieroglyphs – the latter one being your Hidden Hieroglyph (an influence staying in the background that has a subtle, or hidden, influence on you).

Example:

Date of birth – 2 June 1955.

$$
\begin{array}{r}
2 \\
+ \quad 6 \\
\underline{+ \; 1955}
\end{array}
$$

1963 = 1+9+6+3 = **19** (The Sun) – Personality Hieroglyph

You would then add 1+9 = **10** (The Wheel of Life) – Life Hieroglyph

and 1 + 0 = **1** (The Magician) – Hidden Hieroglyph

This would be written 19/10/(1).

Lesson Hieroglyphs

You can calculate lesson hieroglyphs for the past, present and future years. To calculate a lesson hieroglyph, take your birth day and month and add the year you wish to calculate.

Lesson – past

Example:

If your birth date was 19 December 1960, and you wanted to calculate your lesson hieroglyph for the year 1978 (maybe when you started your first job):

$$
\begin{array}{r}
19 \\
+ \quad 12 \\
\underline{+ \; 1978}
\end{array}
$$

2009 = 2+0+0+9 = **11** (Strength) – lesson hieroglyph no. 1

and 1+1= **2** (The High Priestess) – lesson hieroglyph no. 2

This would be written 11/2

Both cards would be the lesson hieroglyphs for that particular year.

Lesson – future

Example:

Using the same birth date as above, now imagine you were planning to get married in 2006 and wanted to check out the lesson hieroglyph that will be accompanying you in that year…

$$19$$
$$+ \quad 12$$
$$\underline{+ \ 2006}$$

2037 = 2+0+3+7 = **12** (the Hanged Man) – lesson hieroglyph no.1

and 1+2 = 3 (the Empress) – lesson hieroglyph no.2

This would be written 12/3

Both cards would be the lesson hieroglyphs for that particular year.

Card 0 (The Fool)

☞*Note: In general, nobody has the card 0 (the Fool) as a personality, life or lesson hieroglyph in this book. Some Tarot books say if your birth date adds up to 22 it means that you have the Fool as your card. This does not apply to the Inner Flame Method. However, since you can choose your hidden hieroglyph, some readers may decide to work and learn from the card 0 (the Fool) as a hidden hieroglyph.*

Chapter 5

UNDERSTANDING THE SPIRITUAL HIEROGLYPHS

You will by now have discovered your Spiritual Hieroglyph (in chapter 3), which will include a court character and a tool. Lets now take a look at what this means for you. Remember, your court character represents you, and the tool is the foundation of your actions and the ruler of your inner patterns.

Section 1 *The Tarot Tools And Their associated Star Signs*

Tools

The tools (rods, cups, swords and pentacles) are described to give you a basic structural idea of their components and energies. For each tool the following information is given

• The associated element (fire, water, air or earth) and its gender

• Season of the year, telling you the best time of the year to apply the inner flame method

• The symbol on our normal playing cards (spades, hearts, clubs and diamonds) to show you how they are depicted on cards today

• Compass point (north, east, south or west) to give you the direction you can face when applying the inner flame method

• Qualities that you can develop or that support you through your life

• Gender (feminine or masculine) to show you the underlying energy influencing the tool that you work with in your life

- Archetypes that the tool represents
- Relevant star signs for each tool

Star Signs

Then we go on to look at the associated star signs in more detail to give you a general idea of the different nuances within the tools and can see what influence the star signs may have on you.

For each star sign the following information is given:

- The star signs associated element and gender.

- Strengths. When writing about the star signs it is important to know the different strengths that they bring with them. Each section mentions their strength as either cardinal, mutable or fixed. Generally it can be said that:

Cardinal signs are strong or forceful energy and carry constructive Forces,

Mutable signs are medium or balanced energy and carry preservative forces,

Fixed signs are weak or subtle energy and carry dissolving forces.

- Stones (or crystals). Stones act as a channel for keeping a focus on your purpose in life. They can also play a healing role. You might, for example, want to place the relevant stone near your cards or carry it in your pocket. It is entirely up to you how you work with the stones. They may be used alongside the hieroglyphs when you meditate – acting as channels for keeping your focus on your inner flame.

- The areas of the soul or physical body that could be affected. This is meant to give you an indication of where you could experience difficulties. Experience show the more you are out of tune with your spiritual purpose or have divided yourself from your good human heart and spiritual inner flame, the more these are the likely areas which could become unstable. If you want to protect yourself from being effected in the particular areas mentioned use the stones named.

RODS (FIRE = masculine energy)

As the fire element, the Rod comes first. All other elements on earth are derived from the energy of fire, which either compresses or concentrates heat.

Season: Summer

Game Cards: Diamonds

Compass point: South

Quality: Passion

Gender: Masculine

Archetype: The Hunter

Star signs: Aries, Leo, Sagittarius

The rod expresses the active and enthusiastic masculine principle. Rod power enables creative form and dynamic self-assertion. The rod represents enterprising and pure spirit, action, growth, life energy, identity, and direction. Heat and light are part of the rod's expression.

When this energy expresses itself in the masculine positively, it is the warrior as a protector. It has the qualities of dynamism, courage, intention, energy, heat, and toughness. In the negative it takes risks, is power hungry, brutal, without feelings and thinks materialistically.

When rod energy expresses itself positively in the feminine, it is independent, optimistic, willing to take risks, self-confident and courageous. Negatively, it is dogmatic, sadistic, condescending, and patronising.

The rod is the symbol of building from a spring of passion. Heat flows through the body and causes an action that regenerates the cells. It is comparable to sun energy. In nature, it is the morning mist.

Rod energy needs constant change and takes initiative when new thought is put into action. Self-trust gives the belief that every obstacle can be surpassed. To sum up the path that rod takes

"All challenges and obstacles can be transformed."

✎Note: Fire is compatible with air and earth.

Fire is antagonistic to water, as water extinguishes fire.

Fire Star Signs

• **Aries** (21 March – 20 April)

Cardinal sign: Constructive force

Parts of the body: Head and face

Stone: Lapis lazuli

Aries lives the beginning. When an idea is born, Aries lives the idea. It is comparable to springtime, and is like the bud that is sprouting. It is the sign where self-unfolding energy is born and it carries the power of bringing into life. Aries allows a lively fire to burn and the secret fire of wisdom to unfold. Aries enjoys starting a project and watching ideas manifest themselves.

Typical characteristics: (positive) Active, strong-willed, self-achieving, adventurous, full of impetus, excited, takes risks, and initiates; (negative) Impatient, self-destructive tendency, problem dealing with own energy, hasty, impatient, fear of confusion or fear of the unknown.

• **Leo** (23 July – 23 August)

Fixed sign: Preservative force

Parts of the body: Heart and spine

Stone: Coral

Leo thrives in the energy of summer heat. Leo is the representation of the secret world. It tends to protect yesterday and tomorrow. Leo doesn't close its eyes and strives towards the light with indestructible awareness and energy. Leo's energy allows it to quickly heal its own wounds. Leo has empathy for others and can deeply penetrate into others' hearts. Leo likes gaining praise for its energy.

Typical characteristics: (positive) Mature, full of energy, extroverted, self-expressive, playful, commands respect, and has strong willpower;

(negative) Excessive self-love, dominant, slow to adjust to new situations.

• **Sagittarius** (23 November – 21 December)

Mutable sign: Dissolving force

Parts of the body: Thighs and hips

Stone: Citrine

Sagittarius can be compared to the winter stillness. It represents the energy of aiming without releasing the arrow (as in Zen mastery). It aims to climb up to an all-embracing consciousness. This sign lives by guidance, following its inner master, which it believes leads it to transfiguration. Sagittarius represents the bridle used to restrain or lead somewhere. It teaches how to be honest about the true self. This sign enjoys its freedom and yearns for more sensitivity in people around it.

Typical characteristics: (positive) Meditative, expansive, self-realising, active, and free spirited; (negative) Inconsistent, difficulty maintaining its ground, and mental coldness.

CUPS (WATER = feminine energy)

This is the essential need of human life to create a body; that which carries life is held in the cups, as the water element.

Season: Spring

Game Cards: Hearts

Compass point: West

Quality: Sensitivity

Gender: Feminine

Archetype: The Goddess

Star signs: Cancer, Scorpio, Pisces

The cup mainly expresses the feminine or passive principle. It represents the world of feelings, compassion, and receptivity. The cup represents happiness, love, beauty, and righteousness. It is the subconscious or the soul. The feelings of loss and grief find an expression here. Its basic energy does not manifest an always visible product.

When cup energy expresses itself positively in the masculine, it is a heart-warming, supportive, and responsive energy. In the negative, it is a chaotic, vacillating and weak-willed energy.

When it expresses itself in the feminine positively, it is healing, spontaneous, giving, full of imagination, and devoted. It is like an angel determined to see the good in all there is. In the negative, it is naïve, dumb and seductive. It also can be devious, fantastic, and destructive.

Cup energy lives in the world of feelings. It is receptive. It listens to the inner voice. It expresses a deep happiness of the heart. In nature, it is renewal and productivity.

It is the place sexuality is birthed. It is the sensuous expression of life, as in a soft flowing landscape of hills covered in wildflowers. Feelings come to the surface in order to allow nature to take its course. The cup's truth is to be what it is, when and how it wants to show itself.

This energy is compassionate with a basic optimistic outlook.

To sum up the path the cup energy takes:

"All things are flowing and any toughness is subdued."

Note: Water is compatible with air and earth.

Water is antagonistic to fire, as fire cannot burn water.

Water Star Signs

• **Cancer** (21 June – 22 July)

Cardinal sign: Constructive force

Parts of the body: Breasts, stomach, womb, and liver

Stone: Amber

Motherhood is born with Cancer. The representation of Cancer is the crab, which is one of the first forms of life on earth. Any ideas are fertilised giving Cancer a creative power. Feelings of the subconscious easily come to the forefront in Cancer. Cancer allows the two poles of passivity and activity to meet and interact. Cancer collects what the heart presents. It is unhampered energy, allowing life to flow as it comes and goes. Cancer's soul lives where earth and water mix.

Typical characteristics: (positive) Enjoys investigating feelings, receptive, changeable, excellent memory, shy, protective instinctive, and open; (negative) Fearful, introverted, easily influenced, tendency to react purely by feelings.

• **Scorpio** (23 October – 22 November)

Fixed sign: Preservative force

Parts of the body: Genitals, rectum, and bladder

Stone: Malachite

Scorpio arrives at the time of the year when plant life is disintegrating. Scorpio expresses this process in life. Scorpio lives in the service of the generations to come. Scorpio is persistent in the action of surviving, going as far as experiencing resurrection during life. Scorpio expresses love through sexuality. It represents the guardian, heightening susceptibility to the subtle energies in the surrounding world. It "ends a climb", because it knows that completion makes new things appear.

Typical characteristics: (positive) Passionate, emotionally intense, excellent survival strategies, healing, and persistent; (negative) Dark, secretive, unforgiving, dependent, creates separation.

• **Pisces** (20 February – 20 March)

Mutable sign: Dissolving force

Parts of the body: Feet, body, aura

Stone: Falcon eye

Pisces lives like the swelling of seeds sown. Pisces can be compared to the cleansing rain. It is adaptable and receptive towards others. Pisces may be withdrawn or indecisive as a result of wavering feelings. It may enjoy mysticism. When Pisces has insights, it may resort to giving them a down-to-earth content. Pisces acts in the name of love and dissolves any boundaries.

Typical characteristics: (positive) Composed, inner power (Native tongue: orenda), sensitive, and patient; (negative) Tendency to with-draw, fluctuating, self-sacrificing, easily upset, dependent, and inse-cure.

SWORDS (AIR = masculine energy)

The next essential need of human life is the medium for movement and the emergence of a life process, which is the sword, or the air ele-ment.

Season: Winter

Game card: Spades

Compass point: East

Quality: Intellect

Gender: Masculine

Archetype: The Elder

Star signs: Aquarius, Gemini, Libra

The sword represents light and clarity. It is power and the fairness of a triumph where mistakes are permitted. Problems are removed. The sword helps to recognise the connection between personal experience and the condition of the world. It is like a butterfly, the completion of the cycle by way of metamorphosis.

The sword represents willpower, understanding, enthusiasm, cour-age, and passion. It is a strong mental energy allowing insight and decision-making. It represents language, intellect, and the world of thoughts.

When this energy expresses itself in the masculine positively, it is intellectual, changeable, alive, and sharp. Negatively, it is cold, reckless, cynical, cruel, and heedless.

When sword energy expresses itself in the feminine positively, it is independent, cool, charming, distanced, and aesthetic. In the negative, it is whorish, calculating, hysterical, and uncompassionate.

The sword is the symbol for strict discipline aimed at constructing without regarding the losses that may occur. It averts dangers. It is the medium which makes things visible. This energy recognises the logic of things. Any deceptions are penetrated in order to uncover the truth. In nature, it may be seen as the whirlwind or the movement of air.

In the mind, it causes the subconscious to work through any structures that create the manifest world. It gains its strength through experiencing difficulties.

The sword cuts through opposition in an attempt to end all differences. It cuts through anyone's truth. Sword energy will sacrifice itself and forget itself, so it needs to be given a direction. To sum up the path the sword takes:

"To be strong without being hard is an acrobatic act."

Note: Air is compatible with fire and water.

Air is antagonistic to earth, as earth stops the air.

Air Star Signs

• **Aquarius** (20 January – 19 February)

Cardinal sign: Constructive force

Parts of the body: Ankles, calves, and blood circulation

Stone: Silver

Aquarius works like an air conditioner. It circulates and cleans all that is no longer serving its purpose for the greater good. Aquarius acts upon its insights. It has an abstract mind, without bias. Aquarius simply is everyone's friend. It represents godly justice and uses its skills, aiming to create utopia. Aquarius dissolves infringing boundaries and thinks multi-dimensionally. Aquarius gets its ideas from the depth of its consciousness.

Typical characteristics: (positive) Observant, decisive, erotic, receptive, spiritual, independent, and talented; (negative) Cold, fanatical, self-sacrificing, and heady.

• **Gemini** (20 May – 22 June)

Fixed sign: Preservative force

Parts of the body: Chest, lungs, arms, hands, and nervous system

Stone: Amethyst

Gemini is born with nature's inherent logic. It welcomes communication of feelings. It has the ability to move intelligently in an orderly and harmonious way. Gemini is open to everything and inventive when it comes to communicating, which enables it to understand duality. Gemini knows the difference between good and bad, but can react ambivalently, because it swings between the two.

Typical characteristics: (positive) Versatile, personable, instinctive, understanding, keen learner, and communicator; (negative) Inconsistent, restless, ambivalent, goes through emotional ups and downs.

• **Libra** (23 September – 22 October)

Mutable sign: Dissolving force

Parts of the body: Kidneys and lower back

Stone: Jasper

Libra lives in the spirit of thanksgiving. Libra knows how to be balanced. For Libra the most important aspects of any partnership are the human aspects. It knows how to compromise. It considers issues and refines its ideas carefully. Libra needs sympathy and friendships. In love issues, it may be idealistic.

Typical characteristics: (positive) Tactful, balanced, intuitive, social, courteous, and aspiring; (negative) Indecisive, frivolous, restless, careless, and parasitical.

PENTACLES (EARTH = feminine energy)

The final essential need of human life is for a foundation, a medium to express and act upon, which is the pentacles, or the earth element.

Season: Autumn

Game cards: Clubs

Compass point: North

Quality: Wisdom

Gender: Feminine

Archetype: The Earth Mother

Star signs: Taurus, Capricorn, Virgo

The pentacle is the combination of all previous symbols. It is the material of earth – real and solid. The pentacle represents humanity, duality, outer life, work, and the experience of the body. It is also material success and practical health as well as home and earth connections. It represents the knot of endless love.

The pentacle is the most human of all geometrical forms. The pentacle energy is faultless in the five senses, the five fingers, and five pure virtues of faithfulness (cleanliness, compassion, courtesy, fellowship, frankness). It is the symbol of balance. Its foundation is feminine wisdom. In the past, only those who wore a pentacle were allowed to enter the realm of light.

When this energy expresses itself in the masculine positively, it is caring, strong and protective. In the negative, it is a stern, strict, aloof, and suppressive.

As a positive feminine energy, it is nourishing, protective, caring, fruitful, forgiving and gives a sense of security. In the negative, it is destructive, possessive, reacts strongly and devours.

It is the everlasting fountain of creativity. Pentacle energy anchors every individual in the real world. It recognises what needs to be done. The magic of earth resides in the pentacle, as well as the capacity to survive. It is magical because it survives. In nature, it is earth, soil, and all life.

Pentacle energy is active and creates consciousness. It lives in love of harmonious change. It mediates in "win or lose" situations. In a materialistic sense, it is not always necessarily good for certain situations.

To sum up the path pentacles energy takes:

"It lives single and free, like a tree on the prairie. At the same time it is a kindred spirit living in the forest."

🔖Note: Earth is compatible with water and fire.

Earth is antagonistic to air, as air attacks the earth.

Earth Star Signs (feminine principle)

• **Capricorn**   (20 December – 21 January)

Cardinal sign: Constructive force

Parts of the body: Knees, skin, bones, and teeth

Stone: Quartz

Capricorn is like the worker in a quarry. Capricorn is ambitious by nature. In order to complete its aspirations, it works through the job and hardly stops. Capricorn sees its ups and downs as a process that keeps it on its toes. It aims to overcome obstructions. Capricorn can be experienced as distant and difficult to fathom.

Typical characteristics: (positive) Concentrated, patient, practical, preserving, and realistic; (negative) Power-hungry, uncontrolled, cool, egoistic, may have sudden tantrums.

• **Taurus** (21 April – 20 June)

Fixed sign: Preservative force

Parts of the body: Neck and throat

Stone: Chrysobal

Taurus is like a farmer working on the field. It gives form to things. It preserves the material and physical world. One can rely on Taurus, because of its solidity. Taurus naturally offers security. It enjoys comfort and administrates any work at hand. In love, Taurus is earthy and sensual. It is a faithful companion.

Typical characteristics: (positive) Strong, patient, manifesting, intuitive, and fertile; (negative) Stubborn, lazy, materialistic, lethargic, given to hidden rage and sudden angry outbursts.

• **Virgo** (24 August – 22 September)

Mutable sign: Dissolving force

Parts of the body: Abdomen and intestines

Stone: Fire Opal

Virgo is like a young, newly sprouting plant. It likes to collect and gather, and then to arrange what it has collected and gathered. It makes a selection and differentiates what is useful from what isn't. Virgo is usually fluent in using and learning languages for the purpose of good communication. Virgo may be overly inclined to serve others.

Typical characteristics: (positive) Analytical, intelligent, healthy, given to classifying, pure, mature, and organised; (negative) Tense, perfectionistic, critical, and cool.

Section 2   Interpretations of Spirtual Hieroglyphs

The Court Cards

We will start with a general look at each type of Spiritual Hieroglyph: King, Queen, Knight, and Page. Next, we will be more specific, looking at them with their tools: King of Rods, King of Cups…and so on.

Be sure to read the general description as well the specific – you will gain greater insight.

Each section will include stories; mythology, philosophies, or religious studies that you may wish to investigate in order to understand yourself more deeply. They may give you deeper insight into the principle that the hieroglyph depicts. I have made references to some of the symbols depicted on the cards where it seemed essential to the particular archetype.

For each spiritual hieroglyph, a stone is also listed. Those who work with the energy of stones find that stones can enhance and strengthen your approach to life.

I have also included two key sentences with each entry: the first gives you a picture of the elements (fire, water, air or earth) involved and how they manifest themselves as energy on earth; the second describes the role you play in life. You may choose to use either or both as affirmations or reminders in everyday life.

THE KING
"I observe"

The king represents the masculine principle. He is self-assured, confident, and active. The king has pure perception, in the sense that he sees right through things and he uses his observational skills to his advantage. He watches from a solid and strong position. He encourages a sense of responsibility in others for his or her "duties" in the world. He aims at completion and retention.

This king's roots lie in the father figure. The king has material power. He shows where the energy of fast and sometimes boisterous activity is birthed. He deals with masculine forces creatively. He communicates with the Great One. He holds the tool (rods, cups, swords, pentacles) in his hand as his source of information. The king hieroglyph is closely related to the Emperor (card 4 of the Major Arcana).

The king's element in nature is fire and his actions are influenced by fiery energy. The king as a role model represents the emotions of the soul. He works with perceiving and solidifying.

His edges may be that he is stubborn, dogmatic, or authoritarian. Sometimes he may be fixated on his aims. His love of control may also express itself in self-control.

King of Rods

The fire of fire is the quick force of an attack – like lightning.

Servant of the Heavenly Chariot of Fire

Stone: Rubin

If the King of Rods is your spiritual hieroglyph, your spiritual purpose is to become an agent of change. You base your intentions on the greater dreams and ideals of humanity while considering past wisdom. You are born with self-confidence and can be compared to a lion, full of energy and passion to fulfill your purpose.

You demonstrate how to stay honest by integrating these qualities intelligently into your soul. You are naturally precise and compassionate. You can be seen vehemently defending an ideal that others may have forgotten, because you have observed that particular ideals are a way to spiritual growth. You represent the impulse to begin and complete projects. Maintaining your personal integrity is very important to you. Some around you may experience this as intolerance. You are a role model for growth and inner development, as it is your purpose to remove obstacles and blocks. You are capable of giving difficult situations a positive direction with a flick of your fingers. Deep inside you are sensuous and sexual. You may act like a snake, which sheds its skin to change and become renewed.

Your motto is:

"Every storm strengthens my roots!"

You bring this pure energetic power into the world as a torch to lead others and yourself to far shores. You generously pour out this energy because it enables you to deal with the darker side of your own impulses. You seek to retain positivity by burning all negativity in an almost ruthless manner.

You are learning to develop sympathy towards your friends or relatives. You may tend to control others by intimidating them. You may be seen as focused on power and prestige, which destroys the creativity of others. However, you gradually develop good rapport with other people, who can act as sensitive advisors to you. These advisors can also prevent you from ignoring "weaker" elements in the world.

You realise the role the third eye plays spiritually. You have the ability to act decisively, triggering further incentive in you and others to complete your task. You experience your energy as an endless force, which makes it difficult for you to stop. You are the kind of person who needs someone or something to stop you. Your fire energy is dynamic and permeates or influences everything you touch. You enjoy mediating and giving moral support. Your thoughts are ruled by:

"Where I am sought – I already am".

Your spirit can be compared to the hot lava in a volcano.

In order to help you understand yourself more deeply, you may find it helpful to study Mars (Roman), an ancient deity, who found his method of keeping enemies away.

King of Cups

The water of fire is the disappearing reflection of an image – like a rainbow.

Charioteer of the Great Waters

Stone: Red Coral

If the King of Cups is your spiritual hieroglyph, your spiritual purpose is to observe your inner life and feelings. This determines your approach to life. You are born with a good sense of intuition. When you don't seek your inner strength, you realise that you could be lead into despair from disappointments that you experience during your lifetime.

You are gifted with an inner strength that gives you the security and support in life to confront the tasks you should fulfill as a king. You may know that you will react spitefully or turn against yourself if your inner life is not retained. In general, your inner life feeds your spirit and it keeps you healthy. Your focus is divided between the present and the future.

You may tend to let others guess what is inside you, and you may be found sitting with a quiet demeanour. You have a subtle presence. You are a born diplomat. You tend to rely on others to enable you to see yourself. You develop an ability to find your centre by being artistic and developing any talents you have naturally brought into life. A King of Cups spirit shows the active energy of water, which is fed by fire.

You may sometimes be lethargic, which results from your intense inner world. You can easily be influenced by others' opinions. Withdrawing from too much activity helps to strengthen you for your duties in the world. Your aim is to look for strength consciously, and then life's disappointments will lessen.

You diffuse any tension arising. When someone attempts to influence or manipulate you, you tend to step back to watch your reaction to the situation. You have the patience to come to your own conclusions before you discuss any further action.

Spiritually, you show your talents willingly, as this expresses your aspiration to reach out to others. Your strength is in seeing right into the heart of matters. You wish to observe both your own and other's reactions to emotional exchange. All your life you strive to experience an emotional exchange with similar thinking people. You also enjoy creating a mental bond with your close friends and relatives. These kinds of experiences kindle enthusiasm in you.

Your spirit can be compared to the warm raindrops that fall during spring or to the water that propels turbines in order to produce electricity.

It may be helpful for you to read the story of Odin (Norse). Odin was a great magician and galloped through the air and over the sea on a magical horse. He developed his inner life and feelings, observed his surroundings, and created interaction.

King of Swords

The air of fire is the consistent power of energy – like the sun.

Charioteer of the Breezes

Stone: Jade

If the King of Swords is your spiritual hieroglyph, your spiritual purpose is to work with conflicts in a spiritual way. Your actions enable you to use your power of authority. You hold your sword as a weapon to threaten those who attempt to threaten you. Using this ability to your advantage means that the queen's role in the court to make decisions becomes irrelevant. Your sword functions as a model of how separation from oneself and from others can be an important asset.

The conclusions you have reached about yourself and your environment give you the ability to keep a clear mind. You have examined your world in terms of causes, motives, and interrelations. You tend to observe and may conclude that conflict will resolve and change a difficult situation. You base your observations on events of the past.

Spiritually you may feel challenged. You protect yourself from other people's insights. You can agree to something and then suddenly decide to do the opposite of what was agreed. You may want to control by threatening lawful punishment. You can react with stubbornness or by being dogmatic. When you defend yourself, you show no fear, as you are born with innate courage, which helps you to develop spiritually.

Your constant mental activity motivates you profoundly. You believe you have a clear purpose in life. You know what you want and may not rest until you have reached your goals. You tend to concentrate on them, not resting until they have reached completion.

Your ideas and thoughts are carried out as quickly as lightning. This shows that you are capable of deeply sensing what needs to be done. However, others don't always understand what you are doing. The may see it as your fixation on action. It is difficult for you to stop, and your spiritual lesson lies in seeking advice from your partner or friend. His or her advice and support make it easier for you to become more sedate.

You are loyal to your inner nature, reliable and open to new ideas. Fundamentally, you are sensuous. You enjoy the company of others and tend to stick to a lifelong partnership. You have a certain amount of headiness that makes you sometimes feel isolated. When you seek advice from your partner or friends on how to deal with your feelings, it becomes easier to relax into your spiritual purpose again.

Your thoughts are based on analysing a situation. You aim to teach people to waive their feelings of security in the roles they play and to lay aside their masks. You also have insights that you share with the world at large. Your approach to thinking is holistic, rather than linear. As a King of Swords, you like to keep your autonomy.

You can be imagined as a charioteer driving a team of galloping horses across the sky. This is how you spiritually cut through your own or other people's set patterns.

Stories about the deity Apollo (Greek) may help you to understand yourself more. Apollo threatened from afar and used oracles for purification.

King of Pentacles

The earth of fire is the power of a volcano.

Landlord of the Wide and Fertile Land

Stone: Pyrite

If the King of Pentacles is your spiritual hieroglyph, your spiritual purpose is to create enthusiasm for producing objects or starting projects in the community. You have earthbound ideas, which you act out on the basis of masculine principles. You put people at ease, making them feel attracted to you. You pay attention to details others would not perceive.

You believe that your influence lies in what you do, rather than in what results out of your actions. You are a hard worker with endless energy and stamina. You stand your ground in the present.

Inside you have exceptional self-control. You tenaciously take things into your own hands. You are a practical person with good organisational skills. Spiritually seen, you radiate a healthy spirit. You induce in other people a sense of material abundance, which you are also striving to create for them.

You may be the person others approach for a diagnosis, as this is something that comes easily to you. At the time of harvest, you are to be found out in the field bringing in the crops. Your spiritual purpose is to show how this is a joyous task for all to share, while emphasising the importance of paying attention to detail.

You may stand in your own way when it comes to showing your inner richness. It can help you to seek help, as this rekindles your sense of belonging to a greater cause. You use all your senses and persevere in order to reach your goals. If your trust is broken, your first impulse is to be merciless towards the offender. Since you enjoy learning, you gradually build up trust again if the offender works diligently towards regaining your trust.

You are learning to balance the masculine and feminine energies in the course of your life. You may have learned to concentrate on material reality as part of your masculine element predominates, so that others can teach you more feminine approaches. When you learn from the feminine, it invokes more creativity in your spirit and expresses itself in your actions. In general, feminine principles enhance your spirit and give you a deeper sense for your purpose in life.

In your approach to life, you can be compared to the energy of fire at earth's core. It may be worth your while to study the knowledge that has been gathered about the earth's core and about its particular function.

THE QUEEN
"I decide"

The queen represents the feminine principle. She is responsive, emotional, and creative. Her purpose is purely to make decisions, based upon the welfare of others. The queen's energy is grounding and earthy. She cares for the safety of herself and others. She protects the family home and the country with an affectionate quality embedded in her soul.

The queen's roots lie in the mother figure. The queen is the creator of material power since she develops and realises the king's power. She projects constant and seemingly indestructible energy. Her actions are subtle, because her main objective is to persevere. The tool in her hand is used to avert dangers from her environment. She is closely related to the High Priestess (card 3 of the Major Arcana).

In nature, the queen's element is water and her actions are influenced by water energy, the realm of feelings. The queen represents the soul. She is responsible for the emergence of a primary energy, which through her presence receives a distinct form.

Her edges may be that she is emotional and lets herself be lead mainly by emotions. She may overpower others with her femininity. She may use others for her own purpose. She may be indulgent and lavish in her way of life.

Queen of Rods

The fire of water is the quick moving, passionate attack – like heavy rains.

Goddess of the Vase of Fire

Stone: Sodalite

If the Queen of Rods is your spiritual hieroglyph, your spiritual purpose is to become a master in self-realisation. Your passions are deeply rooted in your heart. Usually you are full of joy and show a lust for life. You are in contact with your life energy and sensuality. You tend to follow your first impulses, which may mean you live wildly. Your views are based on the present.

You have no problems in stating facts openly in public that others would shy away from expressing. Since you do this in an honest manner, those who gather around you admire you. You realise how important it is to withstand opponents in a decisive manner. You bring along the knowledge that is rooted in looking deeply into your own being. Your spiritual strength lies in steadfastness and developing sympathy.

Spiritually seen, you have intuitive insights. Sometimes you suddenly turn against others, because they do not seem to understand how you developed your views. Then you become impatient or restless. In the course of your life, you are learning to connect yourself with earth in order to keep your feet on the ground. Letting others participate in your spiritual process can assist you to grow.

The Queen of Rods gives the energy to find out what you already know. You act, showing that you know how to act. Then you teach others to have as much knowledge as you already have. You use your knowledge to form your environment. Sometimes this means you become vindictive or power hungry, depending on how others in your environment react to you.

You are a born leader and have had the opportunity to look deep within your soul, either in this life or in past lives – so you gladly accept this role. You exemplify the capacity of fire to burn and give its light; therefore, you give generously and stick persistently to your causes.

You have dynamic feelings, which tend to inspire people around you. You are capable of giving advice, gleaned through your sensitive perception of social circumstances. Spiritually, you grow by keeping an eye on your inner reactions and exploring them in order to continue to grow within.

It may be worth your while to study the story of Kali (Hindu), who proclaimed, "Wherever you seek, I am already there". She acted on the insights of her third eye and protected others from catastrophes.

Queen of Cups

The water of water is the still reflection of an image as reflected in a pond.

Reigning Goddess of the Sea

Stone: Peridot

If your spiritual hieroglyph is the Queen of Cups, your spiritual purpose is to learn all layers of being deeply sensitive. You know the secrets of the emotional world. These deep perceptive qualities give you a clear channel to the feelings of the soul. You naturally regard people around you with compassion. You act to fortify as well as secure others wellbeing, while keeping the past in mind. You thrive by expressing your deeper feelings.

You feel it is your spiritual duty not to make hasty decisions. Instead, you wait and make decisions on the basis of your emotional perception, so they are for the higher good. In this role, you are serene, calming, and true to your feelings at all times – this is part of your spiritual purpose in life. You naturally develop and realise the king's power by providing yourself and others with emotional security. You tend to delegate tasks to the community. You enjoy having a home and a secure network of friends and family, as you are aware that this gives you spiritual stability.

You may give yourself away completely when you share your feelings. This may make you easy to manipulate. You avoid spending time with people who do not understand you, as you want to feel the exchange in communication. You feel hurt if your emotions are not reciprocated.

The energy of the Queen of Cups may cause you to delve into fantasy to escape your depressed side or your rather irrational fears. It may be valuable for you to get support at such times, so that your fantasies may then be transformed into creative actions. You also see emotions as an opportunity to exercise your emotional integrity. In this case, you may require that others take the time to understand the realm of your deep feelings.

You will not accept any compromises regarding feelings, as you know that the root of your reactions derives from the depth of the emotional world, which is more important to you than any other approach.

You may practice meditation in order to become completely still within. You can act as a spiritual guide to those who seek advice. You do this by sharing gathered knowledge about life that could be beneficial for facilitating others' imminent decisions. Especially when you have reached your spiritual potential, you develop an ability to show how material or mental contours and boundaries can be dissolved. You were born with a wonderful glow of light around you, which gives you the ability to present yourself well.

It may help you to get more insight by studying what has been written and hypothesised about the Venus von Willendorf (German) as the feminine symbol of fertility. She is said to have had a deep sense for ancient layers of sensitivity, which play a major role in your life.

Queen of Swords

The air of water is the consistent energy of disintegration – like a sea.

Reigning Queen of the Winds

Stone: Topaz

If the Queen of Swords is your spiritual hieroglyph, your spiritual purpose is to learn to work with ambivalence. In a spiritual sense, you concentrate your attention on detail and seek the accuracy in all things. Often you feel obliged to learn through suffering. You have a deep inner life, which makes you see things others may have never accessed. Your attention is divided between the past and the present.

Your may tend to regurgitate inner processes, which bring up deep fears. You are learning to overcome these fears when they surface by integrating them into your life. You decide in the first instance on what presents itself in the moment; you demand clarity. You may play the following roles in everyday life: the strong mother, the ideal teacher, the bitter widow, the nagging housewife, or the successful businessperson.

You may hide a tendency to be unreliable and cunning. There is often a feeling of restlessness within. With your keenness to gain insights, however, you have developed a clear perception of reality. When you openly speak about what you have perceived, you can change your approach effectively. In general, you have an exceptional sense of fairness when you stand in your power.

You may easily go into isolation rather than accept compromises. You cast hard judgments against yourself. You must protect yourself from becoming too exasperated when your tendency to separate yourself is felt within. The strengths of your good observational talents soften you. Association with a knight enables you to empathize with others.

You are capable of waiving old role patterns. You see how the masks people wear not only protect or camouflage them, but also create a division between themselves and others. Energetically you may decide to cut through these masks, because your goal is clarity in every situation.

You seek a frank exchange of views, which shows your openness and receptivity, as well as your deep, clear wisdom. Your power of thought is unique, as it is not confined by time and space. People who perceive these abilities come to you for advice and guidance.

Your inner processes may cause you to react coldly or by being prejudiced, cynical, and hard to approach. As a result you need caring people around to support you. Your ethos is to ensure that things become manifest without becoming fixed in stone, as this creates your connection to the Great One. You decree that with mental decisiveness you can delve deeply into emotional experiences, which lead you to decide about your next steps. As a result, you act when it is the proper time to act. Your spiritual path can be compared to swallowing the heat of the sun in order to be capable of giving birth to something.

It may be worth your while to study the story of Nut (Egyptian) as mother of the night sky who bent her body over the earth. The purpose of this revered Goddess was to protect autonomy, as well as to evolve by laying masks aside.

Queen of Pentacles

The earth of water is the sensuous power of manifestation represented by the ocean.

Goddess of the Echoing, Soft Flowing Hills and Streams

Stone: Blue Sapphire

If the Queen of Pentacles is your spiritual hieroglyph, your spiritual purpose is to become rooted in your passion for nature. You are connected to an underground stream of water that turns into a spring surfacing on earth. You work hard in order to create a garden, even if it is created out of nothing. You are born with a sound inner foundation. You are inventive because you have a natural ability to live from your centre. You decide with the future in mind.

You react like a mother looking after her children and caring for their welfare. You always show love without expecting it to be returned. You enjoy being in your home, as this nourishes and strengthens your spiritual roots. You enjoy giving your energy away generously. You have a talent to continuously enrich your environment through your work.

The Queen of Pentacle's energy shows how to avoid risks. Your passivity allows things to naturally evolve. You may use your stubborn traits in order to proclaim your deeper spiritual knowledge based in nature's way. Your strengths lie in excellent insights regarding humanity as a whole. You especially recognise different personality types without needing to become acquainted with the particular people. You may be experienced as impulsive but charming.

Sometimes the hieroglyph's energy may cause you to become melancholic and you are honest about this. You are capable of digging into feelings too deeply, but your persistence in this gradually allows you to leave things that you did behind. Standing in your power as a spiritual being, you manifest what makes you feel safe.

You may be compared to the damp clay before it is put into the kiln to bake or to the damp, fertile earth.

From Native American folklore, it may help you to read about the role of Elders in ancient cultures. You can be compared to the spirit grandmother and Mother Earth. You are capable of progressing by spinning a web into the physical world, which to you feels like a sacred act. The spirit grandmother is like the spring from which water exits onto earth. She represents the potential in all things that leads to creation. Mother Earth represents the spirit who created the world. Your spiritual actions lie in acting and teaching others to move through many layers of creation in this way.

THE KNIGHT
"I act"

Knights live combining both masculine and feminine energy. He or she represents action. He or she recognises, acts and takes risks. The knight takes things in his or her hands. The knight takes initiative and gives form. The knight is the charismic master of creative thoughts, ideas, and plans. The knight's roots lie in being a servant figure. The knight acts quickly, but not as sharply as the king. The knight perseveres, but not as much as the queen. The knight's power is diminished if the king and queen do not trigger the knight's actions.

When the knight starts a project, he or she aims at completing its actions. The knight is willing to fight if necessary. The knight holds his or her tool in order to act and find inner strength through carrying it. The knight is capable of acting without someone telling him or her exactly what to do. The knight is the first to take up a weapon when tension arises. The knight is closely related to the Magician (card 1 of the Major Arcana).

The knight relates to the element of air in nature. Moving air, which is the energy of the wind, influences his or her actions. The knight relates well to mental thoughts. He or she has primary energy and works with energy and ego.

The knight's edges may be insensitivity to causing disorder and difficulty in listening. The knight may cause contentiousness without intending it.

Knight of Rods

The fire of air is like a sudden attack mixed with strong winds, as a spreading fire.

Lord of the Spirit of the Flaming Fire

Stone: Moonstone

If the Knight of Rods is your spiritual hieroglyph, your spiritual purpose is to dip into the unknown. This hieroglyph teaches you to do this by contacting the flame of trust deep inside yourself that you know will lead you to spiritual advancement. You naturally allow a space for new things and wish to show others what can be done with them. When you act, you have the future in mind. You have brought along courage and plenty of energy, which you put out into the world. You are strong-willed with a tendency to plough through what has been said, which you then express using new words and thoughts.

To some, you may seem brutal in the way you cut through ties others have made. You may be seen as a figure that appears out of the darkness walking into the limelight. This makes it hard for others to get an idea of your true self. Creating a space to reflect can be helpful in order to let the unknown thrive. When you lose contact with your inner self, you may lose contact with your goals and others may see it as your constant search for new ones. You regain your strength by fuelling it within and reminding yourself of the objective you are striving towards.

Your spiritual power increases when you use all your senses fully. You then stand in alignment with the will of the universe. In general, you are filled to the brim with sensuous feelings and wise thoughts.

Figuratively speaking, you are like a chariot driver who is lead by the glow of a fire into unexpected realms, as this to you is your path to freedom. You are born with intuitive creativity, which makes it easier to radiate your unique intensity. Your uniqueness is that you do not hide or protect your soul from any darkness within. Instead, you react by seeing darkness as an inner power; this can be compared to a phoenix flying out of the ashes. This energy draws you towards your ultimate goal. You are prepared to open your heart at all times. Additionally you have a deep desire to see the world differently.

You enjoy the moments when life touches your inner core. Your general view of life is to see it as anew from second to second. You realise that this power sparks your incentive to quickly move forward. You enjoy conquering new areas in your inner life, as this fuels your passion for life as a whole. Your sense of purpose as a knight is to react to the orders you receive, so that you may lead others conscientiously into unknown worlds. You will naturally open doors to new perspectives again and again during your lifetime.

You may be compared to the moment when gas and air mix as the controlled explosion that causes a car to move forward. When compared to a fire your spirit is the rising smoke.

You may gain more insights from this spiritual archetype in the stories of Krishna (Hindu), who performed miracles, which allowed him to dip into the unknown.

Knight of Cups

The water of air is the ripple of substance that is represented in vibrations.

Herald of the Host of the Sea

Stone: Amber

If your spiritual hieroglyph is the Knight of Cups, your spiritual purpose is to explore the world of desire. You are honest and straightforward about your needs. You are openhearted, while having imagination. Your imagination works as a channel to manifest your wishes in life. You always require a sense that you can return to your inner source. Your actions have the future in mind.

The Knight of Cups represents the most difficult position in the series of spiritual hieroglyphs and as a knight you are the most insecure when action is required. You can be seen as a soft, nonchalant rider on a horse that is mainly lead by your passions. You tend to lose motivation if for some reason your enthusiasm towards fulfilling your desires disintegrates. Your priorities are to perceive and fulfill your passions and desires. Your priority, as someone who is out of touch with reality, is to stay grounded.

Your hieroglyph aims at enabling you to master reaching for the satisfaction of your desires. This requires heightened awareness, as well as intense dedication. These both function as your vehicle into your inner world. It serves you well to focus on life as if it was a poetic play.

You may be inconsiderate, but you generally aim at causing others joy, although when it comes to your own feelings you are reserved. You have a deep wish to be admired, which is authentic and free from the desire to serve your ego. You may be seductive, going as far as smothering people with your emotional power. You tend to evade situations, especially when a person with a king hieroglyph expects you to participate in decision-making.

Underneath, in your soul you are dealing with an ocean where the winds and the waves are rolling. When you or someone close to you has hurt feelings, your first impulse is to disappear from the scene. You may want to learn to examine your intentions by looking at the principles these serve. You aspire to sense deeply that you are following your true feelings and you are willing to look beyond what appears on the surface.

The Knight of Cups energy also represents the ability to master emotional needs. You can be compared to a sailboat skimming over the surface of the sea, which shows that you do not drown in emotions. You are born with a secret hidden power, which is not directly visible. You feel it when you are kept moving, as you truly seek self-improvement.

Figuratively speaking, you are like the cloud that is pregnant with water, but the rain doesn't fall onto the earth. You can be compared to water vaporising. It may be worthwhile for you to study the story of Parzival (Tale by Wolfram von Eschenbach), who was the Emperor king. Parzival went on his journey in search of the Holy Grail, which is similar to the life quest of those represented by the Knight of Cups; stories about visionaries can also help you to understand your purpose.

Knight of Swords

The air of air causes the constant fluctuation of water, which is represented in clouds.

Doorkeeper of the Wild Winds and Soft Breezes

Stone: Hematite and ruby

If your spiritual hieroglyph is the Knight of Swords, your spiritual purpose is to learn all aspects of decisive actions, including being prepared to take risks and to allow radical thinking. You are a master of creative thought, ideas, and plans. You are willing to show aggression, as you do not shy away from challenging situations. You may be described as an active warrior who stands up to dangers. This is a courage that may mislead you as well as helps you along your path. Your actions are taken with the future in mind.

You learn through the assistance and support of others to balance out your first impulses. In your world, any constrictions that inhibit action can be cut through with your sword. In order to give your ideas and plans an expression that others can understand, you can learn to apply various techniques such as visualisations.

You carry the shield alongside your sword as a defensive weapon; others may see this as your fixation on defending yourself. Your challenge is to see that if you get caught up in defensive action for too long, you risk becoming dogmatic or stubborn. You will usually have people around you who warn you of the risk you are taking, so that you invent new methods of action. When there is a confusing situation that others cannot cope with, you have the ability to clarify the whole situation with supreme ease.

You are skilful in action, which may show individual flexibility, but this may also mean you become fanatical in the extreme. You can learn to become aware of yourself as an "intimidating" individual. You can ultimately learn to reflect about your traits. You can learn to bring projects to completion in a different way by listening to other people's advice.

You are learning about the continuous effects of change, which to you can create a sense of the here and now. If you miss stable structures, you should try creating them wherever you can. As you are born with lots of knowledge, you may, for example, enjoy lecturing on topics or giving demonstrations. This may give you a position where you can feel secure in yourself. You are learning to equalise your values, so that you can accept the way things happen. The Knight of Swords' energy represents seeing opposition and acting with bravery to counteract it.

Your purpose is to become conscious of the armour you are wearing and to reflect about its usefulness. You can be described as an active warrior whose aim is to change circumstances that fail to fulfill your purpose.

The myths of Isis (Egyptian) give deeper insights into your ways of fulfilling your spiritual aims. Isis teaches that nothing stays the same and she shows how to balance one's first impulses.

Knight of Pentacles

The earth of air is the manifestation of movement, as in sand.

Judge of the Spirits of Mother Earth

Stone: Onyx

If your spiritual hieroglyph is the Knight of Pentacles, your spiritual purpose is to allow thoughts to develop at your own pace. You are born with an easygoing attitude embedded in your soul that enables you to adjust to the environment whenever necessary. You naturally take care of bodily health and enjoy actively using your body. You act knowing that the future is inevitable.

You have an inbred understanding of natural boundaries and see them in the context of life as a whole. Inside, you have a wish for power, which mainly aims at material prosperity. You are well anchored in yourself. You work hard in an intelligent way.

Your mental power creates objects or projects that have a stable structure. However, they tend to dissolve as soon as you lose the momentum to manifest them. You may be able to complete them if friends or relatives support you.

You may be experienced as greedy and may even be jealous of others. When other people stop you and reflect back to you what effect your reactions have had, you are capable of acting in the name of love. Thus you forget your vices. Sometimes you are seen as someone with willpower of steel.

When you are confronted with environmental issues, you strive to understand these deeply. You may be seen working hard searching for change. You use your abundant knowledge and material wealth practically. You project them into your actions, as would a servant working for humanity. You like assistance when working towards your goals so that things important to you are best done in a co-operative fashion.

You use your natural ability to direct which projects should be completed.

You sometimes may set priorities differently than others. Work may be your main purpose rather than people. You may tend to value people who are of use to you most. You may like to uphold old traditions, as you are aiming at creating a visible product that has accepted qualities in society.

You have the great ability to become a master at combining earth and air energy, although by nature these elements are incompatible.

It can be helpful to study the goddess Athena (Greek), who approached war with a distinctly different attitude.

THE PAGE
"I experience"

The page represents the experience of the effect of actions. The page is the knight's helper. The page lives with both masculine and feminine energy although he or she is predominantly influenced by the masculine principle. The page is active, intuitive, and receptive. The page is willing to try out anything, as he or she is curious by nature. The page is modest and naturally open.

The page's roots lie in the daughter or son figure. The page's power depends on the presence of others. The page becomes conscious of things through experiences in life. The page stands on his or her two feet. The page's tool is designed for self-protection and protection of others and is used mainly as a defensive weapon.

The page relates to the powers of the soul. He or she approaches life with perseverance and self-confidence. The page completes the influence of the court cards and is related to the Fool (card 0 of the Major Arcana) and to the "joker" in modern playing game cards. As a figure in the court, the page tends to shake set patterns, which the king or queen may have set.

The page represents the final movement of energy to form. In nature, the page is closely related to the element of earth and, as a result, grounding energy influences the page's actions.

The page's edges are receptivity and sensitivity. The page may feel hopeless or lose motivation easily.

Page of Rods

The fire of earth is the forceful pressure, which is comparable to the energy in volcanoes.

Red Rose of the Palace of Nature Spirits

Stone: Turquoise

If your spiritual hieroglyph is the Page of Rods, your spiritual purpose is to play with ideas in a spiritual sense. You stay young by working with this energy. You can be found observing growth and turning the sprouting of buds into an experience of a lifetime. This easily facilitates your access to fantastic experiences. You will widely declare the news of your discoveries and experiences to all who care to listen. Your general focus is on the future.

You have an individual beauty, which is comparable to the energy of flames, as it represents the chemical attraction of burnable materials. As a result, you are an individual who reacts with sudden outbursts of being moody/unfaithful or ecstatic/deeply compassionate. Meditative music or playing an instrument like a harp will help you through your process.

You may be seen as superficial or as lacking a sense of responsibility. This derives from your spontaneous anger, or love, since secretly you would also like to rule over others. This is fuelled by your vigorous inner drive towards a leading position. You may courageously step forward in order to reach this goal. Any fears in you are overcome by your fire energy and this enables you to widen your awareness.

You can be compared to the glowing ashes. In your inner world your spirit is like the soft glow of fire which shows as enthusiasm in everyday life. This gives you a fairly consistent character. You know how to live elegantly and in style. You experience sensuality as a natural pleasure.

You learn that you can expand your perception by watching falling leaves floating through the air. You see how each leaf falls differently, and this dissolves any fears you may harbour.

It may be helpful for you to study the story of Pan (Greek), who played the role of the jester to his heart's content while confronting a number of obstacles, and the story of Radha (Hindu) who saw life as a game which she confronted with ease and elegance.

Page of Cups

The water of earth is comparable to the rice paddies.

Goddess of the Deep Waters and the Blossoming Lotus

Stone: Azurite

If your spiritual hieroglyph is the Page of Cups, your spiritual purpose is to become talented in solving psychological or mental problems. You do not get "lost" in solving them all on your own. You have the ability to find different methods to solve them. Figuratively speaking, you demonstrate how to sail to new shores. You are helpful to others. You know how to share constructive solutions that give new impetus to your friends or relatives. Your focus is divided between the past and the present.

By nature, you approach life seriously, while being cheery at the same time. You are born with an independent spirit and a deep sense of responsibility for your own life. This results in less need for assistance than the other pages.

You were born with a sound ability to avoid getting stuck in feelings. As a result, you like to stay away from people who try to get attention for their own purposes. You may conceal the effects your own actions cause, because you are aware of a higher force pulling you on your spiritual path. Your soul wishes to bring about change in any areas of life that you think necessary. Your influence on others is generally hidden, while you tend to dissolve constrictions with great ease.

You are a generous giver and have a soft nature. You are born with a rich imagination, which gives you spiritual inspiration. At times, you may be self-indulgent or a bit lethargic. This develops when you are inactive and is your opportunity to revitalise your spiritual energy. When doing so, you could ask for support from others.

You may be wasteful, for example with money, because to you money can be a means to your spiritual wellbeing. It functions as an opportunity to let your senses command your activities. Your purpose is to exemplify that love is the way to the Great One. You act in the name of love because you want to share it with all those who cross your path.

You reflect about important matters and allow them to come to the surface. You can be found quietly meditating on situations, especially those that have been resolved. The realisations that arise you share willingly, always explaining them in a spiritual context.

You may be compared to the star sign Pisces, who allows the unconscious to rise and become visible. To you therefore the past can be seen clearly, but it can be irrelevant in the present. You act and learn your lessons, imagining yourself surrounded by water. You like dancing a dance of liberation.

You aim at getting manifest energy to transform, so that it is different in its expression. This can be called a crystallisation process. Figuratively seen, you are a rainmaker, striving to crystallise water into ice or snow.

You may want to study myths about Neptune (Roman), who was revered as the God of Fresh Water.

Page of Swords

The air of earth is the consistent carrier of life, as on the plains of the prairies.

The Lotus Flower in the Palace of Air

Stone: Tiger eye

If your spiritual hieroglyph is the Page of Swords, your spiritual purpose is to experience insight in all its guises. One of your main wishes is to maintain intellectual flexibility, as you perceive that many around you use their intellect too rigidly. Others can see this wish expressing itself by the way you act. You are soft and hard at the same time. You strut your stuff without letting yourself be nailed to a role or personality. You trust people and situations. Sometimes you lack an overview about what is really presenting itself to you.

You are curious and wise in your own way. Your observational skills give you inner power. Life to you is an opportunity to remodel and change things on a continuous day-to-day basis. You experience events with the future in mind.

You realise how each of your inner conflicts whirl up clouds of emotions and moods, but this does not prevent you from perceiving clearly. You use your sword to cut through moods and disturbing thoughts within and around you. As a result, you may tend to thoroughly break behavioural norms, because you realise how norms constrict. You also feel that these norms have no real relevance to your approach to life.

Your principle is to say no to obstructions and yes to creation. Thereby you are faithful to your ideals. You may be vengeful, but since you are open to new ideas, this quality is impermanent. You have the capacity to think about complicated states of affairs and this makes you accepted in any environment. It also convinces others around you that you have an important role to play. You learn that looking down on others may destroy social harmony. You could make a point of asking for advice and guidance when life gets complicated.

However, you can also easily let yourself be influenced. As your life progresses you will learn to balance yourself in order to develop beyond the tactics others may apply. You aim at creating new structures. You may tend to want others to think like you do, but are willing to accept that this is not always the case. Your flexibility and versatility enable you to learn different thought patterns.

You may react aggressively to experiences, usually ones you do not understand. The support of others is then advantageous. Gradually during the course of your lifetime, you will learn to balance yourself and to become a grounded person by allowing aggression, but not taking it out on others.

You have ingenious talents when developing practical projects. You have developed wisdom through your insights, but you can carry them a step further, for example, by becoming a counsellor, or a politician.

Spiritually you can be compared to a lotus flower reaching for the sky, creating a connection between heaven and earth. The Hindus revere lotus flowers in their religion, so it may be worth your while to read about the role it plays for them.

Page of Pentacles

The earth of earth is the substance in all its strength, represented by rock.

The Rose Blossom of Mother Earth

Stone: Pearl

If the Page of Pentacles is your spiritual hieroglyph, your spiritual purpose is to develop great respect for knowledge of the past. This can be seen as a gift you were born with, presented to you by Mother Earth. During the course of your lifetime, you honour, investigate and experiment with respect, to your heart's desire. This makes you powerful in a positive sense when confronting challenging situations.

You have a generous and kind nature. You can empathise with anyone who comes your way. You are quiet, not passive. You may be lavish, which in your spirit is experienced as a positive attribute. Your approach to your role is unique.

The earth elements influence you strongly and your first impulse sparks your instant decisiveness. You tend not to care for small details in decision-making. Once a decision is made you want to experience what happens next. Since you thrive on being in a close bond, you may depend on your partner to organise any details regarding plans. You also tend to depend on your partner to make certain decisions for you.

You may feel impelled to give the role of the traditional mother figure a new identity. This is derived from your inner experience that masculine and feminine elements must flow into your personality. Once you internalise your approach, you share it as knowledge and see it as your duty to act on the basis of integrating opposites.

You may be a bit slow or have difficulty in adjusting, as your spiritual nature is anchored in the earth. You are learning how to move within at your own pace. You do not force yourself to evolve quickly. With the assistance and support of other people, you integrate the elements you are missing, that is, fire, water, and air energies.

The foundation of your spiritual activity or purpose can be compared to the effect of magnetic energy, meaning the attraction of magnets, as well as his or her contradictory energy.

The story of Chief Seattle (Native American) can be helpful to study. He served as a role model by showing people how to live in peace for example; he approached the arriving white immigrants with compassion even though he knew they were coming to conquer the land.

Chapter 6

INTERPRETATIONS OF THE PERSONALITY, LIFE AND LESSON HIEROGLYPHS

✳

MAJOR ARCANA CARDS 0–21

Each of the following entries includes a key sentence, which is designed as an affirmation that you could use on a daily basis. It shows your archetype's basic approach to life. Then the keywords are given which I suggest you refer to as reminders of the energies that influence your hieroglyph.

As I have mentioned in the early chapters, I am honouring the work of Eliphas Levi who largely contributed to creating a connection between the Cabala and the Tarot. You will see that with each entry I have included the letter in the Cabala and three keywords to help you understand its meanings. This will give you insight into Levi's approach, and may entice some of you into studying the Cabala alongside the Tarot.

I have also made reference to the Nordic runes (Anglo-Saxon meaning "secret") as many Tarot authors have made connections between them and the Major Arcana deck. These are stones with symbols on them, which up to this day are used as ancient divination stones. If you use runes, they can function as enhancers with your hieroglyphs and also help you to gather more knowledge about different angles and approaches to connecting with your inner flame.

Additionally the areas of the soul or physical body that could be affected are stated. This is meant to give you an indication of where you could experience difficulties. My experience is that the more you are out of tune with your spiritual purpose or the more you have divided yourself from your good human heart and spiritual inner flame, the more these are the "likely" areas which could become unstable.

As this book is designed to give you the incentive to learn more about the knowledge that has been gathered in the past, each section also includes stories, mythology or philosophies that you may wish to investigate in order to understand yourself more deeply. I suggest looking at the Suggested Reading at the back of the book, too.

With the inner flame method let me remind you that the Fool (0) is not a personality, life or lesson hieroglyph. However, since the Fool has links to other cards in the Major Arcana it could be useful in certain situations. For example, the Fool functions as a hidden hieroglyph and it is also mentioned within some of the interpretations that follow because its energy influences some of the hieroglyphs.

0 ✳ The Fool

"I am nothing."

Keywords: The freedom-seeker, the juggler, the wanderer

Cabala: Tav

Keywords: Goodness, the lap, a formation

Rune: Wunjo

Keywords: Alignment, bliss, joy

Effects on the soul/physical body: Deficiencies or weaknesses, such as anaemia, or osteoporosis

This hieroglyph's main focus is on learning the art of nothingness. Your spirit may feel it has not yet started its journey or that it is in a state of inertia. For you, there are no rigid systems and no guidelines to follow. Inside there is a natural knowingness that everything is in motion, however, the direction and the result of the motion is unpredictable.

You have an innate ability to carelessly spread joy and share your lust for life. Sometimes this means you may have no immediate sense of direction. Symbolically the Fool stands for detachment from worldly things. The Fool's motto is:

"I am without a beginning nor do I have an end, I am older than the day and the night. I am younger than a baby. I am brighter than light, darker than darkness, beyond all objects, and live in everyone's heart. All this is in me!"

This hieroglyph shows you how to act like the immortal wanderer, who can be found everywhere. You have a sack full of ideas. You may enjoy disturbing structures, which in your opinion are too rigid. In everyday life you may sometimes speak out loudly. You enjoy acting like a gateway, in creating something out of nothing. You enjoy the simplicity of just being alive. The Fool's role in the court of past days was also to remind humans of their mortality and you have deep inner knowing about this.

It may be helpful when your spirit is stuck to work with Pluto energy. Pluto represents the protector of treasures and acts as the generation planet. Pluto teaches that the one who goes behind, goes in front. This energy can allow your life juices to flow freely again.

The Fool hieroglyph represents a constant state of unusually deep and at the same time foolish wisdom. It functions as a buffer to help friends or relatives protect themselves from developing excessive pride. When you show your deep and foolish wisdom, it often reveals a deep desire in anyone you meet to live like a gypsy. This is your way of showing others how to integrate the various experiences that lie in the Major Arcana as a whole.

The Fool loves the mystical and has the potential of always being ecstatic. Additionally you feel comfortable when sharing the insights derived from playing this role. You have made investigations into mystical truths that teach humans to become ecstatic about creation. Your inner flame reacts to life, as it is "in the moment," so that spontaneity is a natural asset to you.

The hieroglyph's energy can be compared to the spirit of ether, which stands for an abundance of wisdom, yet it is etheric, or invisible. The Fool's motto is:

"Let hazard be your friend!"

You usually see the truth others can't recognise. It causes you to feel like you are somehow standing at a crossroads, where everything begins and everything ends.

1 ✳ The Magician

"I am."

Keywords: The clown, the connoisseur of rules, Yang energy

Cabala: Aleph

Keywords: The nature of God, the ox, energy

Rune: Fehu

Keywords: Cattle, ownership, peace, cosmic fire

Effect on the soul/physical body: Immune system

The Magician focuses you on expressing creativity while using your innate ability to simultaneously apply your intellect. This enables you to complete your actions with plenty of skill and imagination. You succeed because you have been given the ability to thoroughly examine your inner being. This hieroglyph stands for infinity and is a symbol of continually flowing movement in life, as well as of godly balance.

In general, you have an active and positive attitude towards existence. You take initiative while keeping a distinct self-awareness. You may often feel you must "juggle" or move things around in order to reach a solution. On most cards, the four tools are laid out in front of the Magician. All these elements (rods, cups, swords and pentacles) are yours to carefully balance, especially when it is important to act in a decisive way. This hieroglyph gives you a view of ordinary life that is unique. As a result, you teach others the advantage of rejuvenation as part of life. You show people that if they are willing to shed their skin like a snake, this unleashes a different approach to being human.

Your focus is to juggle with material and spirit in a magical way. You are also willing to struggle with dark mass in a spiritual sense and aim to set free any hidden light. The wand the Magician holds on most cards is the tool of your creative power. This shows that you can work with the law of polarity and make others see that counteracting forces exist for all forces in the universe. Some may revere you for doing this, while others may see you as distant and cool. Your spirit is free of corruption, since it is full of creative powers that transform any negativity.

The hieroglyph's energy empowers you within. You are led to integrate magic gradually, so that it becomes part of your expression. You learn to see that you must be careful not to disperse your energy in all directions, or you will lose your centre. You should aim to develop a good inner balance. Your path to success is based on the experience you gain from developing interdependence.

You seek your truth by learning to understand the inner nature of reality. The first step is to attempt to overcome any contradictions you might perceive. Then you can learn to understand that contradictions exist because humans have been separated from nature.

You stand in the centre of life by allowing the heat of the sun to enter your spirit. You are learning that the sun centres the human body with its heat. To you the sun represents your psyche. You can play with this energy and then initiate those around you into a hidden world of knowledge. This is how the hieroglyph teaches you to create a connection back to nature and to let go of the polarities you have let yourself be ruled by. These two myths describe your hieroglyph very well: The story of Osiris, who represented the essence of the God to which everything returns and of Horus, as his son, who commanded the skies.

2 ✳ The High Priestess

"I am thinking."

Keywords: Passivity, self-confidence, the woman's church

Cabala: Bet

Keywords: House, Goddess of Fertility, the mouth of humans

Rune: Uruz

Keywords: The aurochs, rain, duality

Effect on the soul/physical body: Spasms or too much in the mind

The High Priestess focuses you into expressing and developing feminine power effectively. Your wish is to become a guardian of this power. You are born with a beauty that inspires and attracts others to you. The hieroglyph shows you that higher knowledge is within, creating a link between the emotional and mental world. The next step is to balance any contradictions you may perceive in those worlds. Before you take action, you know the importance of meditating first.

By practicing modesty, compassion, and patience, you are lead by this hieroglyph to recognise things others do not see. It more or less orders you to get many of your inspirations from meditation or inner listening. Then you can advise your friends and relatives to look inside themselves, to think thoroughly, to act sensibly and to ensure that they are firmly grounded. This hieroglyph makes clear to all that although one can wear a mask by day, at night the dream worlds unlock one's disguise. Thus you are empowered to aim at waking up whatever is asleep, because it is important to remove the veils that mask deeper emotional layers.

The edges of this hieroglyph are that you may feel insecure, vindictive, or intolerant. Your actions may incline to fanaticism. Because of these inclinations, you may refrain from putting your feelings into action. You know that in order to develop insights you must overcome resistances within. Your spirit is striving towards freedom by gradually reaching reconciliation with your fate.

In numerology the number two is an echo, a shadow or basic matter. This can be the path for developing your feminine power, so that you can stand in your power. It includes all memory, imagination, psychic forces, and spiritual wisdom. You deal with the deepest part within your soul. To you, your soul lives and expresses itself in your body, which feels like a temple to you.

Altogether, the High Priestess hieroglyph embodies internal strength and harmony. You think life through in a clear and sharp way. You analyse in black and white with the authority of a wise woman and spread the feeling that each is part of the whole. The hieroglyph makes you work with the contradictory forces of feelings that arise, which may mean expressing or creating confusion. This is part of the process to reaching feminine wisdom. The hieroglyph ensures that you act intelligently with a certain degree of soberness.

In Chinese philosophy Yin energy, meaning feminine energy, provides the food for the soul. An open attitude towards everything is important. Yin energy means that if you give yourself, with patience, the world will reveal itself. You dedicate yourself to the energies behind the mask in order to activate Yin. You have a fountain of reserves, which you can naturally draw upon.

If you wish to learn more about this hieroglyph read the story of Artemis (Greek), which gives an in-depth account of how to become a High Priestess, a shaman, and the story of Amazona (Roman), who was a wild woman who lived according to the feminine principles.

3 ✴ The Empress

"I feel deeply."

Keywords: The source of existence, loyalty, nature

Cabala: Gimel

Keywords: Nature, fertility, Friday

Rune: Thurisaz

Keywords: A giant, a doorway, eternal return

Effect on the soul/physical body: Blood system or hormones (possibly infertility)

The essence of the Empress hieroglyph is to fully display the feminine way of life to the outside world. The energy of the Wise Woman and the Virgin were given to you. Your spirit expresses sovereignty, and gives energy that makes you young at heart, because you use your purity as a path to redemption. On most cards, the Empress carries a shield. This is available to you when expressing your aims. The shield is the symbol of the sky and depicts the Godly triangle (Egyptian): thought (Osiris), value (Isis) and spirit (Horus).

This hieroglyph wants you to act as a catalyst for the Great Mother image, which balances the manifest world and the forces of nature. Also, on most cards the Empress is carrying a sceptre in her left hand, which here is meant as a defensive weapon, signifying protection.

This hieroglyph naturally imparts the energy of safety, security, and vitality with an inbred intelligence. You have been given the gift of observation and the ability to understand, which enables you to feel at home in this world. You have a treasure of deep feelings and compassion. You have the receptivity of a woman, which involves understanding how important it is to be in a continuum in the rhythm of life. You learn and practise the art of giving birth to life, new ideas, or projects.

The Empress's limitations may be a tendency to suddenly deviate into the abstract when discussing issues. You can become vain. You may have an inclination to splendour and luxury, which can be expressed in extravagance. This could lead you into trouble in material matters.

You are learning to guard yourself from your own exaggerated feelings as you progress in life. You receive inexhaustible strength and your mind becomes active in many directions. Your spirit learns to deal with feelings by digesting them and then applying the lessons in everyday life. It is no coincidence that others observe this process in you because it is something you wish to master in a spiritual sense.

In any case, the hieroglyph gives you an ability to fill your world with joy while you lead your own fulfilled life. You tend to enjoy the protection of a partnership. The Empress energy can be compared to an amateur gardener, who with love, care and toil enables the garden to prosper. The Empress also often endows you with a psychic ability, which can attract searching souls.

It may be worthwhile for you to study the story of Aphrodite (Greek). Aphrodite was the Goddess of love, passion, and beauty. She nourished a fire in her heart. Although she tore the collar around her neck to save her favourite lover, this action helped to strengthen the bond between them. Also, the story of Cassandra (Greek) describes another aspect of this hieroglyph. Cassandra foresaw the fall of Troy, which rescued the people from experiencing an unexpected disaster. As a result, Cassandra was never revered for her prophetic qualities, but she was worshipped.

4 ✳ The Emperor

"I prevail."

Keywords: The window, "Vivat. Crecat. Floreat" (Latin: "Live. Prosper. Flourish"), higher intelligence

Cabala: Dalet

Keywords: Knowledge, the seat of thoughts and feelings, Thursday

Rune: Ansuz

Keywords: A God, the stag, communication.

Effect on the soul/physical body: Abdomen

The Emperor hieroglyph focuses on your unique power over the material world. You feel that you must actively show this power to the world. As a result, others will see you as a capable governor. The hieroglyph gives you the ability to use your intelligence – in combination with an acquired position – as your means to pull strings. You represent the source of constructive work.

Instead of acting in the feminine as the High Priestess (Card 2) does, you receive masculine energy. As part of the masculine energy, you realise that you have the power to destroy and preserve. The hieroglyph shows you that self-control leads to the completion of a task and you embody a strong sense of responsibility.

The energy of this card makes you act like one who rules in his or her kingdom. Your task is to be like a relay station, which distributes energies from a higher to a lower level. This will enable you to take life in your stride. It is an opportunity to develop your awareness, so that you can learn to strive towards happiness in life. Generally, you have an optimistic spirit.

This hieroglyph's edges may be in pushing you to wish to misuse your power; others can experience this as dark dictatorship. You may become unbalanced, which means risking chaos. You may ignore intrusions you think will suppress your masculine approach. Although this may mean that you turn a deaf ear to the benevolence or compassion of others, you receive the energy through this hieroglyph to develop a sound ability to learn and to open to new horizons.

Jupiter energy is very helpful to the Emperor hieroglyph because it teaches that there is a time for everything and that all will unfold at the right moment. It gives energy to allow positivity into your life. The moment you integrate Jupiter energy it adds an extra-ordinary quality to your life. Jupiter also gives you the strength to extend or expand actions in a just way. You can learn to use Jupiter energy for widening your awareness and for releasing your vices. Jupiter enables you to see the way ahead. It gives the incentive to see that willpower is a key factor in dealing with Emperor energy.

Generally, you can be felt as a stable element since you successfully conquer demands and disturbances as they arise. You are regarded as a master of your trade. You may feel that you must subordinate your feelings because of your obligation to see things objectively. At this point, you would gain from advice from those around you.

Your sexuality is mainly governed by a wish to create life. You feel an inner obligation to represent the masculine archetype. You also represent the quality of courage. The numerological definition of the number four means stability, or materialisation. This shows that as a masculine archetype, the Emperor must stand for certain principles and can also defend his position freely.

The throne of the Egyptian Pharaohs, who controlled law enforcement, symbolically represented the visible and invisible laws on which all laws are based. You sit, metaphorically speaking, on the throne in order to bring these laws into the real world.

Studying the story of Hercules (Greek-Roman) can be helpful. Hercules, who was usually shown holding a bow or club, was a determined man, full of energy. He stood steadfast in his power. It was only when it was absolutely necessary that he enforced laws and then he was always prepared to accept the consequences of his actions.

5 ✳ The Hierophant

"I unite. "

Keywords: Inauguration, faith, clarity

Cabala: Heh

Keywords: To breathe, strength, feminine spirit

Rune: Raidho

Keywords: The chariots, ritual, manifestation

Effect on the soul/physical body: Skin or respiratory problems

The Hierophant hieroglyph focuses on your inherent natural wisdom. Your wish is to experience all that this entails. The hieroglyph's strength comes from the masculine realm, which lies in being active. The Hierophant energy conveys insights into the mysteries of life. You feel you should teach others to take time for mental and moral development. The energy drives you to actively introduce ideas and behavioural patterns. You are learning to represent the equilibrium that arises from balancing internal aims and outer obligations.

This hieroglyph takes the mental stages of humans a step further. Here it is not sufficient to want (card 1 Magician), to mentally analyse and recognise (card 2 High Priestess), to feel (card 3 Empress), and to show strength (card 4 Emperor), rather it is necessary to have the will and the ability to unite opposites in order to adapt or to harmonise with the higher teachings. As a result, its goal is to birth new ideas, thoughts, feelings, and observations. The Hierophant hieroglyph encourages you to achieve a balance between your inner urges and your outer duties. It acts like a bridge builder.

The hieroglyph's edges may mean that you are superstitious. You also may be excessively proud of yourself. Sometimes you can lead others astray because you take advantage of your acquired abilities. Others may see you as a tireless adventurer, or as a compulsive dogmatic.

The energy of Saturn can help you to develop further. Saturn is the guardian of the threshold that hinders and delays movement. Saturn shifts the spirit with sudden change. It facilitates maintaining life wisely. Saturn's energy thus makes it easier for you to release your pride or superstitions.

This hieroglyph shows you how to be kind. It gives the ability to forgive and to apologise if necessary. You are willing to make personal sacrifices. You create harmony wherever possible. Your motto is:

"There is only one message that is worth listening to – the one of my heart."

On most cards, the Hierophant is holding a staff. You are asked to use the energy of the staff to create the connection between above and below. The hieroglyph gives you a complete and natural sense of how to convert your ideas or insights into words. You may openly express religious teachings, acting according to them. You may also help to overcome the problems of others if they step forward. You draw your sexuality from the feminine by being aware of the role that sensuality or passion plays. You are well balanced in your thinking and bring light into darkness when necessary.

The crossed keys on most cards symbolise your emphasis on community. You learn to define the hidden messages of life and pass these on verbally. Most cards depict the Hierophant sitting in front of a curtain. This indicates that you may open the curtain to the hidden realm when you feel this could lead someone to a profounder understanding of life.

This hieroglyph naturally connects you to human intuition, wisdom, and the rational mind. You know about the Great One's lessons, which give you the ability to see things with higher consciousness. You teach widely on this basis. Your lesson is to become adept at uniting different fields of thought, explaining them holistically.

It may be worthwhile for you to study the life of the Buddha (Buddhism), which describes this hieroglyph's focus.

6 ✳ The Lovers

"I decide on an inner level."

Keywords: Beauty, selection, inner balance

Cabala: Vav

Keywords: Liberty, the eye and the ear, children

Rune: Kenaz

Keywords: Fire, desire, burning torch

Effect on the soul/physical body: Difficulty feeling rooted in life

The Lover's hieroglyph focuses you in making decisions on an inner level. You do not wish to feel pulled in two directions, which constantly seem to attract you. This energy gives you the sense that although it seems a difficult task, you wish to succeed in making clear inner decisions. The hieroglyph focus shows you how to derive a sense of your own undeveloped or unlived side, and through this you learn to confront temptations.

On most of the cards, a man stands between two attractive women. The role of the women is to mirror him, so that he sees the reflection of his own soul condition in them. You are impelled to begin searching for what you realise is missing. Then you notice that you grow from seeing yourself being mirrored. You realise that the women make it possible for you to develop anew. You may tend to use this process as an opportunity to unfold your true willpower, but also you may see it as an endurance test leading to progress in life.

Your edges appear because of your inexperience, you react immaturely or indecisively. You may then try to escape from your challenges by being insincere or selfish. You may also feel discontent with those around you when you allow your fears and doubts to take over. The hieroglyph's energy makes you cautious, as you may think you are making a premature decision. When you give in to this, life causes you to feel helpless or inactive.

The energy of the planet Mercury in its purest form can facilitate the hieroglyph's process. This planet teaches that form and shape, in the mental and intellectual sense, hold everything together. Mercury creates high mental abilities. Mercury also shows the mysteries of the energies inherent to the universe. Thus, your soul learns to communicate with this in mind and gradually replaces your edges with love.

This hieroglyph shows you the path to follow in order to solve many unresolved problems. Along the way, you become aware that you may encounter many challenges and temptations. You learn to become conscious of relationships and the magnetic strength of opposing forces, which you encounter in life. Yet, the hieroglyph gives you the ability to see beauty in everything, big or small.

When you internalise the limitations of body, intellect, emotions, and spirituality, you reach independence, since the completion of the process entails transformation. In this sense, you learn to act in your own enlightened manner and to receive higher consciousness. Having internalised the steps, you become capable of confronting life out of your own power. You learn to live in the spirit of the marriage of masculine and feminine. The hieroglyph's energy strives to push you into acting under the formula that two are necessary, so that one can become acquainted with another. This is the means to attaining the light.

Read the legend about Hercules (Greek), as it is a good example of your process. Hercules had the choice between two qualities: virtue and lethargy. By his crucial activity, he developed a sense for his goal and balanced the inner and the outer of his nature.

7 ✲ The Chariot

"I am moving onwards."

Keywords: To triumph, to advance, to learn

Cabala: Zayin

Keywords: Ownership, the arrow, tools

Rune: Hagalaz

Keywords: Hail, the Shaker, radical interruption.

Effects on the soul/physical body: Depression or moodiness

The Chariot hieroglyph focuses on broadening your line of action into the physical, intellectual, and mental spheres. This spiritual driving force determines the path you are taking in life. Along the way you learn to set limits and you learn to keep yourself under control whenever it appears necessary. You become determined to strive towards a destination only you can create or see.

The hieroglyph shows that at certain times in life human beings can experience inner strife or deadlock. You are given the ability to teach yourself and others to continue the journey boldly, regardless of limitations. You may then proclaim that challenges in life are to be accepted. For you sometimes a departure, a separation, an internal and/or outer journey must take place. In your soul an inner realisation is developing that a rigid structure, routine or completed task in your or other people's lives should be broken.

The hieroglyph's edge is that it may be difficult for you to accept the humdrum of ordinary life. This may be because you lack tactical intuition; instead, you may want to bury yourself in intellectual pursuits, which give you a reputation in society. However, if you internalise the Chariot's lesson properly, it means that you stop short when it is time for a big change and begin by steering your life in a different direction.

The energy of Capricorn helps you to learn to be honest and to breach the challenging aspects of your inner life. The Capricorn winter sky opens the most beautiful perspectives. The maturation process of Capricorn is to be free from desires on earth. This gives you an ability to control your desires and apply them as if you were guided.

The hieroglyph generously endows you with adaptive skills. You become empowered to consciously see your path and willingly strut your stuff. Whatever restricts you, you will leave behind. Your challenge in life is to lose your fears by no longer suppressing your inner drive to keep your pace.

Symbolically the Chariot shows how to surrender to the laws of the Great One who teaches and enacts the principle of defence against lower forces such as death. You apply your intelligence and physical knowledge well. You may use your body and intellect as a means to higher awareness whilst aiming at securing a position in society that suits your requirements. You have the ability to overcome challenges on a day-to-day basis; this prevents you from becoming stuck.

This hieroglyph teaches you to convert thought into action. You learn to take control of your feelings. You become courageous. Some may see you as overcoming your fear of dying. However you must be in balance in mind, body, and feelings; and see in your true position in the scheme of things.

The Chariot hieroglyph can be compared to the shaman's path. Therefore it may be worthwhile for you to study books about shamanism. In Egyptian legends, the deeper meaning of this card appears in the legend of Osiris. The Chariot of Osiris showed that all plans could be carried out, if the four wheels and the two horses were steered accurately in the chosen direction.

8 ✳ Justice

✍Note: Some Tarot decks number the Justice card either 8 or 11. In this book, the process described is an inner process, therefore it is numbered 8. But you may want to read both descriptions (cards 8 and 11) and decide for yourself which card resonates with you. If you decide that your hieroglyph is Strength, then please feel free to apply that hieroglyph instead of this one.

"I balance myself."

Keywords: Order, conscience, peace

Cabala: Het

Keywords: Fences of protection, animals, plants

Rune: Nauthiz

Keywords: Need, pain, restriction

Effects on the soul/physical body: Circulation problems or low energy

The Justice hieroglyph teaches you to avoid extremes in everyday life. Its spiritual energy aims at creating a sense of balance in life. You learn to evade extremes while setting your mind on achieving the balance. It acts as a helper to make you feel centred. The hieroglyph takes the energy and lesson of the Fool (0) one step further – which is to wait before making an immediate or careless decision. It provides the awareness that great ideas should be realised, not minor ones.

This hieroglyph can teach you to reflect regularly on daily situations by taking time to do so. It is an energy that focuses on the necessity of balance when balance has been interrupted. You are empowered to create harmony. Sometimes this means that a retreat for a period of time is advisable in order to face inner needs. The purpose of this period is to rediscover balance.

The edges of the hieroglyph may cause you to react aggressively, showing the imbalances that you see or feel. Thus you may ask that a re-examination take place. You may request corrections. Others may react by saying you are self-tormenting or egoistic. You may remind them that one is free to do everything; however, it is important to ensure that situations are balanced. This hieroglyph ensures that responsibility is taken for the consequences of all actions.

Your guiding principle is that one must first look at a situation objectively and then reflect on all sides of the issue, before a balance can be found. This course of action also opens channels for learning to control negative emotions differently. It reminds all who come in contact with it of the art of impartiality. In this sense, you can see this hieroglyph as either an obstacle or a protective wall.

After reflecting about a situation, you have the courage to face challenges, and life takes on a new quality. In essence, you let fears of imbalance dissipate. You are being taught to give birth to your real self. This is your form of aligning with nature.

Additionally, the Justice hieroglyph wants you to integrate the masculine and feminine elements into your life. It allows you to see how nature changes. In order to understand nature better, you may tend to suggest that elements of nature could be regarded separately. If there were an argument, you would tend to let everyone speak and be heard in order to seek a solution that balances all people's wishes.

The number eight on the card is the symbol of infinity. In this hieroglyph, this energy represents the inner path to equilibrium.

On most cards there is a woman holding scales. This can be interpreted as representing the Yin/Yang (Chinese) principle. If you wish to learn more about the Justice card, it can help to study this Chinese symbol.

9 ✺ The Hermit

"I am content with myself."

Keywords: The pilgrim, the wise one, the search

Cabala: Tet

Keywords: Creativity, the roof, foundation

Rune: Isa

Keywords: Ice, inertia, cooling down, standstill

Effects on the soul/physical body: Ulcers or overactive mind

The Hermit hieroglyph focuses on allowing the reflection of your soul to be shown in a new light. It shows you how looking into yourself can bring insights. It begins by stating it is important to see light within. The light activates clarity, so that every second of your life becomes a conscious moment. You mature with what you see and react by gradually finding an inner sense of wholeness for the greater good.

This hieroglyph's energy can be compared to a growing tree, which soaks in water, so that it can mature. You work with this as follows:

"I am content with myself and I trust my path to self-knowledge. Noises, fearful reactions around me, or shouting crowds do not affect me, since I am feeding myself and this is how I continue to prosper like a tree."

The Hermit hieroglyph may cause you to feel bitterness about what you see. Your words may become harsh, as you suffer from a certain inner rigidity that can develop from this process. Others may think you have become strange because you abstain from worldly actions. You need the incentive, or a trigger, from people around you to get out of your self-made cave. Your spirit is a dream carrier.

The hieroglyph teaches that by leaving the isolation of your cave and allowing relationships, you become capable of dealing with your spiritual lessons creatively. You bide your time, however, in order to learn to trust your internal healer. Hermit energy focuses you gradually on learning to listen to your inner voice.

You may begin by decoding your insights. The number nine in connection with this hieroglyph symbolises hibernation before a new beginning. As you mature, you gain more knowledge about the secrets of emotions. You tend to look for truths while being shielded from the outside world. You develop your ability to "hunt like an owl at moonlight"; that is, you get deeper insights from your dreams. You may separate yourself from society with the deep inner knowing that you will return as a teacher or role model.

The light the Hermit carries on most cards, is the ancient symbol of the Great One, who passed on teachings to humanity. It makes you a patient, almost silent warrior. The hieroglyph shows you how to do profound work and to master things not all see. You want to become the being you were chosen to become. Instinctively you follow an inspiration that lights up your path. Thus the hieroglyph helps you to find your wholeness, to look ahead and never look back.

The story of Nemesis (Greek) as the distributor of happiness and despair can be worthwhile for you to study. Natives or Aboriginals, who go on vision quests or on walkabouts, also exemplify this hieroglyph's way of thriving.

10 ✵ Wheel of Life

"I am creating a balance."

Keywords: Inventiveness, ambition, vitality

Cabala: Yod

Keywords: Divine spark, the heroes, framework

Rune: Jera

Keywords: Harvest, Fortuna (Roman: goddess of luck), Jupiter

Effects on the soul/physical body: Throat or lungs

The Wheel of Life hieroglyph focuses your spirit into the process of movement, which infiltrates your life positively. It is teaching you to link to changes and movements as part of the moment. You learn to focus on seeing life as an eternal new beginning and therefore nothing ever stays the same for you. The hieroglyph also shows you that considering different or new approaches is always worthwhile; this enables you to feel grounded.

The presence of the Wheel of Life hieroglyph encourages you to understand that nothing is certain, except uncertainty. Numerology defines the number ten as the symbol of the wonders of the world. The four elements on most cards are at your disposal as your wonders of the world, showing you how to keep a balance in your personality. The elements show the following processes, which you may learn: The mind masters fire energy by being creative, water energy by allowing feelings to flow, air energy by allowing liberty and earth energy by developing accuracy in actions. You may master your feelings by becoming balanced through warmth (fire), compassion (water), openness (air), stability and loyalty (earth). Your willpower will grow through becoming infused with an objective (fire), adaptability (water), openheartedness (air), and through your ability to create mass (earth).

This hieroglyph's edges are that you may become inconsistent. You may be aware of a certain amount of innocence within, which may bring a danger of losing yourself. You may feel like you are getting lost in a labyrinth or you may be unable to protect your own personal identity. If you allow yourself to learn, you will see that fate teaches you self-reflection and wisdom.

You may not understand life's lessons in the first instance. Yet through the four elements, you can learn to succumb to the course of life. This hieroglyph's energy keeps on refreshing you. You are given the gift of learning how to confront fate instead of trying to escape from it.

The Wheel of Life also teaches you how you can change the direction and the speed you take in life. The most important questions for you during your lifetime are:

" What does happiness mean to me?"

"What obstructs my path to happiness?"

The hieroglyph shows that each time you find the answers to these questions you are closer to the centre of the wheel, and the negative influence of the wheel is reduced. The Wheel of Life shows you when you are out of balance, or when you feel ups and downs, like riding on a quickly moving Ferris wheel. You utilise the gifts of human willpower, understanding, and feelings in order to return to your centre. Your goal is to be in the centre of the wheel, which in the Wheel of Life means acquiring the ability to follow the movement of what is happening around you.

On most cards, a hand appears out of nowhere. This is the hand of the Great One. It acts as a protective influence and takes away any pain or suffering. The Great One requires that you do not insist on security while He turns the wheel. In the Egyptian legends, the sphinx (symbol of feelings) was the entity who clearly knew that higher beings observe and lead everything.

The Wheel of Life is usually depicted with twelve spokes. These are reminding you of the astrological signs and the energy of the planets involved in human development. One star sign that may be useful in your process is Capricorn. This star sign teaches you to experience unexpected changes as a free play of forces and gives a grounding element to your own balancing act. In regard to the planets, Pluto fills you with an abundance of energy, and Jupiter is a generous bringer of happiness.

This whole energetic experience tends to turn into an inner, personal matter for you during your lifetime. In hours of darkness, light enters your soul. Any person who is influenced by the Wheel of Life is continuously learning all aspects of non-attachment.

Buddhist teachings about non-attachment can help you to understand this hieroglyph better.

11 ✳ Strength

☞Note: Some Tarot decks have the Strength card as number 8. In this book, it is numbered 11, since the principle of this hieroglyph is an event triggered by an outer process. Read both descriptions (cards 8 and 11) and decide which hieroglyph resonates with you. If you decide that your hieroglyph is Justice (card 8 in this book) then please feel free to apply that hieroglyph instead of this one.

"I tame my instincts within."

Keywords: Inner magical power, the solution to a problem, determination

Cabala: Caph

Keywords: Mars, the helping hand, first movement

Rune: Sowilu

Keywords: Sun, life forces, wholeness

Effects on the soul/physical body: Infections, bladder, or liver problems

The main focus of the Strength hieroglyph is the experience of walking along life's path in order to confront "beastly" instincts that you normally cannot control. To you they feel like a force that exists outside of your control. The hieroglyph empowers you to develop an inner moral strength, which enables you to overcome these instincts. You learn about all the ins and outs of instincts first by developing new energy. Then this process allows the fear you feel to spiral into compassion towards his or her existence. You learn to love the strengths you have, even if your personal attitude towards them is negative.

Often the card shows a woman holding an animal at her side. The hieroglyph wants you to see the raw power of this animal as an incentive to treat yourself to taming and gaining insights from your instincts. You may learn to predict when you feel you must follow your instincts instead of succumbing to them. You may be empowered to see that shortsightedness brings failures. The Strength hieroglyph is paving the way to winning this inner battle.

You gradually realise that the hieroglyph's edge is your love of power, which derives from the process you are experiencing. You may be inclined to show outbreaks of rage when you are not allowed to use your power. The way you express yourself may cause others to feel you are being cruel. By following the law of polarity, you can have the courage to see your edges. You must work towards integrating your masculine aggressive side. In numerology the number 11 is defined as secret, as in nature it is said to be an invisible number. This is an indication pointing you beyond form into the eternal.

When the eleven is added (1+1=2), the High Priestess is your balancing energy. Your whole inner being can become infused with a dynamic strength through her subtle presence. You can learn to act with the still composure of the High Priestess, which may enable you to stand in society allowing continuous renewal to flow. As a result, you do not know the word impossible.

This card teaches you that blockages are a reflection of outer circumstances, and accepting this as a fact leads you to great splendour. When the inner beast is tamed and integrated through your affirmation and devotion, it becomes a companion. You then allow energy to flow because you have learnt that any energy is an enemy as long as it is not loved. Furthermore, you recognise that your thoughts of imbalance are incorrect. Instead, you live by declaring that there is a way to create balance. The hieroglyph gifts you with mediation skills in order to create the balance necessary.

It can be helpful to study the planet Mars for the purpose of understanding this process. Mars has the energy of growth, giving an initiative to "dare" to change. It also gives the patience to learn about anger. Mars enables such raw and crude energy to become stronger, so that the hieroglyph's energy is able to serve its purpose.

12 ⚹ The Hanged Man

"I see the world upside down."

Keywords: Powerlessness, identity crisis, disillusionment

Cabala: Lamed

Keywords: The victim, learning, Saturday

Rune: Tiwaz

Keywords: Justice, peace sign, renewal

Effects on the soul/physical body: Tumours

The Hanged Man hieroglyph focuses you on allowing creative phases in your life to unfold. Spiritually seen, you allow an examination to take place. The hieroglyph pushes you by an outer influence into the upside down position. This shows how there is a mysterious force outside of your control causing a defensive reaction. You may become passive and through the passivity discover your active side. In some cases, complete inaction may result. You sacrifice yourself because this way the mind is brought to a standstill.

Your lesson is to accept reality and at the same time not to deny your needs, wishes and aspirations. In this case, the planet Uranus allows you to shed the veils that have covered your eyes. Uranus represents the quantum leap. Although the leap may be frightening, it turns into an excellent asset. It may take time for you to realise what effects the denial of reality have had on the whole of your life; often the results of the gained insights may not show up until the second half of your life.

The Hanged Man hieroglyph warns that you may not be able to free yourself from the pressure of activity. If you allow too much blood into your head, you may develop a feeling of hopelessness. Hanging upside down also may cause apathy. The passivity or inactivity you display, however, should not last for a long time. It should be just long enough for you to reach conclusions. It facilitates your letting go in order to rearrange your future.

Ask others to assist you in finding equilibrium. You learn to understand that your liberation comes after suffering, through the sacrifices you are making. Saturn helps your process, as it seeks to give wisdom and peace. It also supports you in approaching obstacles as a discipline, which then nourishes your integrity. In numerology the number 12 is regarded as multiple lunar wisdom, so that the moon could intensify this hieroglyph's urge to allow creative change.

Another connection is to the Bible, which says that descending into darkness leads to redemption. As a result, if you feel like a victim you can break out of old patterns. You know that by doing this a correction can be made. The action of turning upside down gives you the liberty to release earlier belief systems. Deep passions can be overcome; meaning symbolically that when a lock in a canal is opened, deep feelings are released.

You may benefit from reading the story of Odin (Norse) because it tells how he sacrificed himself. Also the story of Perseus (Greek), who flew over bad forces to release himself from imprisonment, creates a connection that can help you to understand this hieroglyph more deeply.

13 ✸ Death

"I transform."

Keywords: Renouncement, relativity, renewal

Cabala: Mem

Keywords: Wisdom, woman, transition

Rune: Birkana

Keywords: The Birch Goddess, Nut (Egyptian), boat

Effects on the soul/physical body: Fevers, respiratory or skin problems

The Death hieroglyph focuses you on renewing through allowing death processes to occur. It empowers you to know that death means transformation. You learn that by permitting death to happen, you can be reborn into a new life full of possibilities. You go through life using this as a stepping-stone to opening one door after another. Looking back, you see each closed door behind you as an end to an epoch. This hieroglyph's energy teaches you to regard new situations audaciously. It gives you the ability to work with faith and doubt or luck and misfortune, as if they were one and the same thing. To you, to possess means to lose.

The hieroglyph proclaims that the very moment that psychological fears are permitted to come to the surface, a birth takes place that allows them to die. Then you and those who listen to you will be in a new place where change becomes possible and inevitable. The Egyptians defined number 13 as the number of completion. To you this would mean that nature puts order and structure into the world through the transformation, which is exactly what you want to learn.

The hieroglyph's edge is that clarity is not always an advantage. It shows you inertia is connected to this path. You may have doubts about your insights. It then becomes difficult for you to let things die or transform. Old habits can prevent you from seeing death as transformation. The constant experience of death or transformation can lead you to feeling weary or despondent and as a result, you may want to try to escape from the feelings that it causes.

The star sign of Scorpio helps you to appreciate death's gift and to allow this gift to become part of your spiritual purpose. Scorpio energy also gives you hope and optimism about what death offers. Here death is showing how sudden pain can occur outside of your influence. You will want to share the anguish, pain and fear this causes. Even when you feel exhausted, you nevertheless can change the feeling into optimism. You will wish to have death affirmed as a means to an increased awareness of life in the moment.

This hieroglyph proclaims that life can be felt differently once you have permitted your heart and soul to see that life is not eternal. It wants to discourage linear thinking. It will assist you in understanding the separation that needs to take place. Influenced by its energy you will teach others to look into the world and to watch how death occurs, for example, in nature. You experience life as the natural unfolding of nature and your advice to others is to follow suit. Therefore, the Death hieroglyph shows that individual existence is no longer absolute.

The story of Prometheus (Greek) may be worthwhile for you to study, as it tells how Prometheus went about succumbing to death.

14 ✶ Temperance

"I renew the mixture."

Keywords: The seasons, versatility, reconciliation

Cabala: Nun

Keywords: Relapse, a fruit, Sunday,

Rune: Lauguz

Keywords: Water, initiation, tides

Effects on the soul/physical body: Tendency to infections

The Temperance hieroglyph focuses on creating the right recipe for you in life. It teaches you to develop; that if you pour any ingredients from one container into another you produce a new mixture with a new consistency. You *tend* to work with the mixture diligently in life, since this turns into your form of practice. Therefore, you learn to step out of isolation or limitations, allowing new experiences, or mixtures, to surface in your life. This leads you to eventually become more spontaneous, relying less on security.

Your process is to learn to release energy in order to become active. Start by controlling your mental impulses. This permits you to be open to flexibility. Since the thoughts about the ingredients, or the form, can require your complete attention, you may become preoccupied with this and nothing else. This may cause you to lose the ability to make decisions. However, as soon as you turn towards the world, you change because it allows you to create anew.

Perhaps the energy of Temperance may force you to contemplate for a period of time since you wish harmony in all situations. You learn to see that harmony cannot be forced into existence just by a flick of your fingers. With this process, you allow events to flow, which allows your spirit to reach more consciousness. The star sign of Aquarius shows you how to live your dark side. Aquarians learn from the time of snow thaw. This time of the year enables the balance between the outer and inner impulses to change. As a result, rigid obligations that were followed in the past may expire and be dissolved into a healthier process. Then you will no longer swing between moderation and extremes.

As with magnets: where the attraction and repulsion of energy mutually cancel each other out, so this hieroglyph teaches you to internalise the ability to compromise. It becomes an essential element in your life. You are also being taught that a "short coffee break" is important, since a break sets creative energy free in order to reach balance. The hieroglyph takes the lessons of the Lovers (card 6) lessons on to another stage, by uniting and allowing things to become whole in this present moment.

Most cards show a woman with two vessels, who pours liquid. This action can be compared to granules running through an hourglass. The vessels are usually made of different materials. The gold one represents the sun, standing for the principle of action, and the silver represents the moon, standing for the principle of reflection. To mix these opposite energies is an alchemist's task. An alchemist transforms base metal into gold. He should not spill anything. This teaches you that changing does not mean losing your special individuality, rather it is re-enforced, and the final product becomes an integrated synthesis.

Any information or stories about alchemy can help you to understand this hieroglyph. The myth about Ares (Greek), the god of war, can help you to see a different strategy is possible.

15 ✳ The Devil

"I have too much of one and too little of another."

Keywords: Ambition, commitment, temptation

Cabala: Samech

Keywords: Rest and contentment, Mercury, Wednesday

Rune: Algiz

Keywords: Moss, protection, defence

Effects on the soul/physical body: Lung or respiratory problems, nervous tension or cramps

The Devil hieroglyph teaches you how to learn about and follow your instincts. In order to master your instincts you naturally cut yourself off from attachments and blindly fall into activity. The Devil is a symbol of the divisions people experience. However, it acts in order to lead you out of dead ends, which you may feel are splitting you apart. On one hand you feel deep inside that you have no influence on the course of your life, and on the other, you are well aware of what you are doing as the hieroglyph pushes you into activity.

The hieroglyph can pull you into blind passion. Your passion forces can show you how light enters darkness. You are realising that energies harbouring in your soul must find an expression in order to introduce change, and allow you to follow your instincts without incurring damage.

The number 15 is the number of sexuality and the senses. Surrender to circumstances you cannot influence. This will give you an energy boost, so that you are open, for example, to satisfying your sensuous desires. You will learn to know and teach others exactly how materialism can be deceptive. By exposing yourself to passion, you may feel transformed and a new horizon may appear.

This hieroglyph's edges are that you may become cruel or superficial. You may also feel that you have been robbed of your own will. Your reactions to these "negative" impulses may mean that you become uncertain or even despondent. But that is only a temporary state. In the end, there is nothing that can stop you. The hieroglyph provides you with a natural sense of humour as a tool; for example, you apply humour when there is any confusion that prevents others from being instinctive. You can learn from integrating the energy of the planet Mars. Mars signifies the primeval urge of spring. Mars teaches the flow towards renewal and gives an eloquence to handle integration. Also it is an energy form that propels or accelerates processes. Thus Mars shows how to be determined and how to induce change.

You are also learning to change your urges into useful tools. By integrating these lessons, the traces of your actions no longer destroy anything in your environment. The Devil card shows the opposite process to the Lovers (card 6), instead of striving for paradise it shows the best way to go through hell. The Egyptians taught that whoever wants to go highest must go through the deepest. Your spirit confronts the darkness, so that in the long run you release becoming over-identified with the mask of the ego.

Study the story of Pan (Greek). Pan enticed all those around him with his music, so they gave up their social norms. He wanted them to allow their secret wishes to come to the surface. The myths of Dionysus (Greek) may also be helpful. Dionysus, who was possessed by devil energy, shook the people awake; as a liberator, he encouraged others to let go of old structures and conventions.

16 ✳ The Tower

"I release in order to renew myself."

Keywords: Subversion, boldness, intuitive flash

Cabala: Ayin

Keywords: Equilibrium, tools, Monday

Rune: Yr

Keywords: Inner peace movement

Effects to the soul/physical body: Digestive or circulatory problems

The Tower hieroglyph teaches you all aspects of dealing with soul changes. The ego, which includes attitudes, pride, vices, etc., is unmasked. This process begins with a feeling of constriction and the wish to expose what is underneath.

Two significant things are shown on the Tower hieroglyph. People are seen falling out of the Tower and lightning has struck it, causing a fire. This suggests how to work with destructive forces. On the card, the windows of the Tower are open to the outside world; they make you aware that when an external force hits, you can act. You also learn that if you don't find the inside stairs of the tower, you must, figuratively speaking, fall down the outside.

Your spirit is eager for significant shifts. Your attention is on unexpected breakdowns, as you feel that long-established patterns are not eternal. It does not suit your spirit to be in a safe place, as it causes you to feel imprisoned.

Seen from outside, this energy appears painful, but for the person living in this energy, it is the best way to move. You act as a role model for allowing corrections in life to be made. You know that refraining from corrections can cause failure. You show how to turn towards new approaches in life and cut ties with the past. Any flaws appear to you as opportunities, where you or others can rebuild. In this way, you show how to unmask the structures of the ego.

Since the hieroglyph causes you to shake things, you may be intolerant towards those who don't take this approach. Also your spiritual energy may make you feel imbalanced and your learning process may be difficult to internalise. This process gives you the energy to integrate – figuratively speaking – your spiritual purpose into the driving lesson you are taking.

The Tower hieroglyph represents untiring and dynamic striving for self-confirmation, that is, for success, power, safety, warmth, or security. This means that you may feel that your life force is spilling over or an explosion is necessary to set yourself free. The hieroglyph gifts you with the capacity of mastering extreme forces, so that the release of suppressed energies affects you positively.

This hieroglyph seems to impel you to erect unreachable heights, which cut you off from nature. Sometimes you cannot open the channels to nature. You visibly get stuck. You also are learning to understand other people's outlooks on life and this becomes a discipline you wish to learn. You may reach out for help and perhaps someone will help you to jump gracefully. Either way, the Tower hieroglyph facilitates your return to nature. It helps you to open doors, to feel more grounded.

It may be useful for you to study Faust (Goethe), who was learning to arouse, heal and reconstruct the parts of his identity that were hidden inside himself. In mythology, it can be worth your while to study Odin (Norse), or Mentu (Egyptian).

17 ✸ The Star

"I set creativity free."

Keywords: Self-realisation, wider consciousness, inner harmony

Cabala: Phei

Keywords: Opening up, tongue, fire element

Rune: Ehwaz

Keywords: The "holy" horse, defensive forces, new growth

Effects to the soul/physical body: Overloaded mind or heart problems (maybe addictions)

The Star hieroglyph focuses you on sharing and teaching the forces of peace and equilibrium. You demonstrate that stars are alive in everyone and that the knowledge of the universe is at everyone's side. This hieroglyph's energy shows how the stars nourish you. You are gifted with faith, as your love for beauty comes from your connection to the stars. You naturally use your curiosity in order to bring their knowledge down to earth. Under the influence of this hieroglyph, you learn to radiate inner harmony.

This hieroglyph shows you how to create a healthy relationship between work and play. When you are working, you learn to convert your tasks into play. This means an infinite abundance of ideas bubble into your work. Your efforts at work can be of great benefit to all. What you are learning gradually creates the self-confidence to maintain a healthy relationship towards work and play.

The energy of the hieroglyph may cause you to become sensitive to energies that oppose your purpose; so the planet Venus is a helpful companion. Venus is the planet of love and harmony. It can teach your spirit to sing a song of thanksgiving for the beauty that encircles life. It enables you to comprehend and appreciate what is available from living this way. As a result, you learn by drawing on your strengths and by using your intellect.

The Star hieroglyph leads you on the path of creative strength. You are learning to act playfully. It allows new things to be discovered or forgotten things to be rediscovered. This is how you gain realisations. It also enables the flow of your actions to begin to appear, so that growth is set into motion.

Many clear insights arise from learning this hieroglyph's focus. As a result, limitless possibilities for self-development arise. You may experience this as light, which suddenly enters and releases the willingness to do different things.

On some cards, eight big and four small stars are depicted. The eight big stars are defined as the new beginning of infinite possibilities, meaning that you are learning to develop optimism. The four small stars symbolise the possibility of developing what is at your disposal.

Most cards show a naked woman. Her nakedness makes clear that the hieroglyph concerns the whole person. She represents the daughter of creation, the renewal through faith and hope. Her action of pouring liquid back and forth aims at passing on various energies to the universe; for example, the liquid purifies the world of terror and destruction. This means that spiritually you can return to caring for the universe, through cleansing the negative and working towards positive thinking, and a revival of sensing and feeling. The story of Ganymede (Greek) is worthwhile studying because he served the Olympic Gods. Zeus appeared as an eagle and kidnapped Ganymede, taking him to Mt. Olympus where his work changed into play.

18 ✳ The Moon

"I look deeply into the soul."

Keywords: Night, sentimentality, sensitivity

Cabala: Tzaddik

Keywords: The roof, the dream, shadow, and reflection

Rune: Odila

Keywords: Inherited land, the back of the head, the mysterious

Effects to the soul/physical body: Moodiness, melancholy, fever, or colds

The Moon hieroglyph spiritually works and plays with the energy of the unconscious. The moon shines at night, so at night you can search in your soul for useful ideas that will help you along life's path. You receive dreams or take time to reflect at night so as to change the thoughts, feelings, or actions ahead. The moon reflects sunlight into the darkness of the night – in this sense you are working or playing with the light of the night.

Energy of this kind brings psychological and mysterious forces to the surface. You can become passionately attached or enchanted by these energies. It is important for you to analyse your experiences of the darker side of life.

Most Moon cards show a crab and a dog (or coyote). The crab is defined as the animal of the subconscious and the creative power of water. It represents a teacher that shows how subconscious elements can become recognisable. The crab, one of the first life forms on earth, lives between earth and water. The crab's process of digesting its food while living between earth and water represents your ability to morally regenerate.

The dog (or coyote) is defined as the guardian of the underworld and is a symbol of belief because it is a faithful companion. It also represents the fiery energy inside your soul. Its presence reminds you to guard the willpower in your soul, which is in danger of being taken away from you.

You may remain in a state of enchantment with Moon energy. The hieroglyph may cause you to become aimless or lethargic; as daytime approaches, you sometimes would prefer the night to return. The Moon has a subtle tendency to pull you into its force. Also you may become fearful from dreams or insights. But these experiences enable you to learn to see your fears as warnings, without withdrawing from the daytime. Your task is to convert the ideas you receive from the night, putting them into creative action. This hieroglyph acts like a stepping-stone to a new level of presence during the day. You may also strive to dissolve fears.

The hieroglyph teaches you that you may not have the immediately recognisable goals that others may expect. It helps you to be mysterious, especially when temptations or challenges present themselves. You have an inner devotion to serve by learning to lose certain attitudes and you show a willingness to serve the greater good. You discard prejudices because the moon's influence enables you to wash them away.

Moon energy causes you to experience the process of rebirth. Any fears that are brought to the surface are cleared during the night. You learn to deal with deception. At night, you go to the darkest places in your soul.

Your process can be compared to the menstrual cycle of women, who cleanse their bodies by bleeding every month, which in this case represents the liberated force of the feminine. It enables you to do rituals in order to attain the power of prophecy. Thus you express your mystical knowledge to the world.

These are the ways this process may affect you:

Hecate's way (Greek): You experience the realm of darkness. You fall and sink into it. You do not emerge from it without help and support from others.

Selena's way (Greek): You react gently, in a feminine way. You uncover deceit and look more deeply into self-deception.

Diana's way (Roman): You master the art of hunting, this means you realise you can decide to hunt, if this is what needs to be done, or you watch a hunt unfold.

Studying the stories and myths of these goddesses may help you to understand this hieroglyph's focus.

19 ✻ The Sun

"I see the light."

Keywords: Flourishing life, gold, daytime

Cabala: Koof

Keywords: Soul life, laughter, earth element

Rune: Gebo

Keywords: Giving, partnership, fusion

Effects to the soul/physical body: Rheumatism or general circulatory problems

The Sun hieroglyph focuses you on the means to change and to work with changes as a life purpose. Your actions are based on the power of love. Your path is to show yourself and others how all things in life are connected. You know that there are limitations to actions; these often are symbolically depicted on Sun cards by a wall. You tend to use the heat of the sun as your guide and the wall as the boundary of your activities.

Your spirit has two totally different worldviews. You stand back to watch the connection between the inner and outer movements of humanity. This way you learn to master intermingling forces. Another theme in your life is communication. The card takes the lesson of the Wheel of Life (10) into completion. As you are learning to communicate, you are being taught that the mystery of life is not a problem that needs a solution; rather it is a reality, which must be experienced. Your energy is aimed at reaching freedom from opposing forces by amalgamating them. This hieroglyph thus teaches you to understand that life is full of opportunities.

The Sun hieroglyph may cause difficulties when people around you react to the heat you emit. Others may feel you are burning them inside or you may experience burn out. When you learn to understand the reactions this hieroglyph can cause, you will see the importance of communicating with others or learning to love your heat, so that others develop a liking for you. The star sign Gemini enables you to realise your goals. This star sign begins at the time of the year when the sun is at its highest point. Gemini represents life bursting-open, and nature getting the impetus to mature. This is the moment when insights show a positive and negative aspect. You react by aiming at integrating both sides into your soul, so as to feel free. Usually two people, just like the star sign of Gemini, appear on the Sun card. This signifies that a human being has two sides, which interact and communicate as masculine and feminine entities. You thus reach your centre by allowing these opposites to become partners.

The light of the sun represents the essence of clarity. Your soul realises that this can become your means to higher awareness. You see that it is your choice whether or not you work with this energy. Once you have begun integrating all aspects of this hieroglyph, you walk through life aiming at becoming enlightened, but this is not something you do consciously.

When working with the Sun, it may help you to read the many stories about the Unicorn. The Unicorn brought joy and also enabled people to rediscover their inner light. The myths of Helios (Greek) as the God of the Sun can also be helpful.

20 ✳ Judgment

"My desires are fulfilled."

Keywords: Resurrection, rebirth, intuition.

Cabala: Reisch

Keywords: Eternal life, gratitude, war and peace

Rune: Perth

Keywords: A dice-cup, secrets, the hidden lessons

Effects to the soul/physical body: Lymph or blood system

The Judgment hieroglyph focuses you on the fate of earth. It becomes one of your main concerns. You are fulfilled in yourself and tend to teach others how to break connections with old traditions, values, judgments, etc. The hieroglyph brings deeper knowledge of how humans pass through stages to reach greater awareness, making transformation possible. Desiring completion, you also seek to solve the questions of existence, by changing any worldviews that may have become irrelevant for you. The hieroglyph's energy creates the wish in you to aim at fulfillment. At each stage, you can easily review your path and change direction, while asking yourself the following questions:

" What have I done? What have I done wrong? Was I unfair?"

The answers to these questions enable you to progress to other areas where you are capable of taking responsibility for your life.

The edges of the Judgment card are that you may have difficulty finding happiness. You may become discontent. But deep inside you realise that this comes from your own misinterpretations of the world. You may take this as an incentive to become more honest about yourself by following an invisible path, taking a direction that suits your needs. This card facilitates your ability to truly understand other human beings in all their contradictory behaviours.

As a result, the hieroglyph brings you forgiveness as a gift. You discard any garbage that you feel burdens you or prevents your inner happiness. With such a fresh approach, you discover joy. The number twenty is the number of demand. It makes you endeavour for the better. It thus initiates new currents.

The Judgment card often depicts six people. This is a reference to the family that is around you, as well as to the lessons and teaching of the Lovers (card 6). In this case, your inner call is to raise yourself in a spiritual sense beyond the inner plane, to a spiritual purpose ruled by human fate as a whole.

The energy of the planet Pluto helps you to find the path into the world of splendour. Pluto teaches you to initiate a cleansing process of fire and water. Pluto has growth as its foundation and its effect can appear beyond today's generation. In this case, it means the Judgment hieroglyph transforms thought patterns for your spiritual well-being and for the well-being of others who cross your path.

It may be worthwhile for you to read the story of Aeon (Greek). As the Sun God, he demonstrates this process by dying at night and being born again the next morning.

21 ✳ The World

"I open the door to reveal paradise."

Keywords: Unity, self-realisation, all the senses

Cabala: Shin

Keywords: Intelligence, the arrow, the Great One

Rune: Gibor (hidden Rune, do not use without the guidance of a professional!)

Keywords: Humans become one with the Great One, conception, total loss of ego

Effects to the soul/physical body: Bone or skin problems

The World hieroglyph focuses your spiritual being on striving to consolidate the experiences of past generations. This hieroglyph forces you to experience consciously the role of an observer. It teaches you that the way to provide the insights into the inner and outer reality of being human is to carry past experiences into the world. Thus your life becomes a reflection of a new world opening up and enabling you to grow.

This hieroglyph brings to completion the lessons and teachings of the Judgment card (20). It supports you in identifying all forms and boundaries of eternal life and it prevents you from becoming too self-involved.

Fatalism or self-destructiveness can affect this hieroglyph when expressing its aim. As you are fighting against outer circumstances, you learn that self-criticism and change in your approach to life can free you of difficulties. Integrate your own changes by surrendering, as it may show you how to become adaptable.

You may begin by turning what you give to others into devotional love. The moment stark contrasts are overcome, you forgive or unite them. You also learn the need to return from chaos to a point of stillness.

The World hieroglyph teaches you to welcome the perfect solution by enjoying the present moment. This may be a deeply satisfying experience. Obstacles are obstacles no more. You are uplifted and can dance the dance of joy and thanksgiving. Your spirit can bless others. This hieroglyph wants you to share the results with a celebration. You can be like a creator and perform the dance of life in its purest form. You perfect anything that was begun before you.

This hieroglyph's counterpart is the Fool (card 0), who acts as a subtle partner, or hidden hieroglyph. The difference between the two is that the Fool represents innocence while the World hieroglyph embodies maturity. Together they spiritually lead to ecstatic paradise.

It may be helpful for you to study the story of Gaia (Greek), as the Goddess (or the personification) of Mother Earth. She was born out of the void of emptiness within the universe. It may also be worth your while to look into Native American wisdom on the fox.

Chapter 7

THE GUIDANCE HIEROGLYPHS

✴

ACE – 10 OF THE MINOR ARCANA

Section 1 – Introduction to the Guidance Hieroglyphs

In this book, the 40 numbered cards of the Minor Arcana are the guidance hieroglyphs. There are four different groups of cards: rods, cups, swords and pentacles, and each series consists of ten cards, numbered Ace – 10.

Let's start by investigating the numerological aspects of the 40 cards. The number 40 is defined as a celebration, a wedding, or the time of newborn things. For the Inner Flame method, this is the overall energy that influences the complete series of the guidance hieroglyphs.

It can be said that generally the Minor Arcana hieroglyphs show the different types of experiences and feelings you may have in the course of your lifetime. The cards depict ideal, or pure situations, which you will experience at some point in time. They are pictures of all the possibilities of human expression. It is therefore inevitable that you will experience these situations.

Guidance hieroglyphs are exactly what they say – they give you channels for guidance. They teach you to observe, feel, think, and experience by guiding you to the knowledge of the masters in ancient times. Each set of ten cards shows the path that each experience in life takes under the aspect of the tool. With the Inner Flame method this path functions like a gateway, or doorway. This can be seen as the process of moving from potential energy to kinetic energy.

Each set of Ace – 10 shows the path the tool takes as a natural law of evolution. The processes described on the hieroglyphs for the Inner Flame method can be seen as stepping-stones to deepening your understanding of experiences.

For the Inner Flame method the guidance hieroglyphs:

- facilitate answers to questions by giving guidance
- give deeper knowledge of experiences in life
- facilitate experiences so they come to the surface
- allow experiences to flow, or to open the heart
- open inner blockages to a process not experienced before
- break patterns
- work as channels of change

The ancient Tarot books explain Ace – 10 cards in many ways. Let's look at the numerological meanings given to the numbers of the Minor Arcana cards for the particular purpose of this method.

Numerological meanings at a glance:

Cards numbered 1 – 4

(cardinal numbers) Introduce the process. They represent the material work and carry forceful energy.

Cards numbered 5 – 7

(mutable numbers) Strengthen/preserve the process. They represent the lower astral plane and carry balancing energy.

Cards numbered 8 – 10

(fixed numbers) Seed change in a process. They represent the higher astral plane and carry subtle energy.

Number 1 – The undivided unit, signifying the possibility of something manifesting, and opening the doorway into an experience. It represents the opportunity of beginning anew. The essential abilities of the four hieroglyphs of the 1-series are: the seed of creative ideas (rod = fire), the seed of feelings (cups = water), the seed of thoughts (swords = air), and the seed of materialisation or action (pentacles = earth).

Number 2 – The encounter or the mix of 1+1=2, which represents duality. The wisdom that resides in this energy must join before an outcome can be reached. It is an energy form representing the first exchange or encounter. The four hieroglyphs of the 2-series are the different ways an opinion can be formed.

Number 3 – The exchange or the blending of energy. This energy counterpoises the contradiction that is inherent to duality. This energy introduces a new element by showing how ideas can manifest. The four hieroglyphs of the 3-series generally show how duality is balanced. Each hieroglyph represents the opportunities and challenges you can face in life.

Number 4 – The recovery phase, describing a boundary you may confront. The energy facilitates wholeness. The four hieroglyphs of the 4-series show different expressions of moments of inspiration, and show you the different opportunities to consolidate or prepare for something new.

Number 5 – The moment of proper refinement, or the dissolution of the human position through opposing elements. This energy describes the moment before you continue on your path, especially when it becomes necessary to complete a process in your soul. The four hieroglyphs of the 5-series represent the types of opportunities or challenges that can be expected.

Number 6 – The "spark" of new energy showing how a different type of balance happens in comparison to the 3-series. This represents the moment of refinement and takes the energy of the 3-series one step further. In the 6-series, the energy is transformed into the integration of mind and material. This energy represents the provocation that keeps a relationship alive. Each of the hieroglyphs shows how decisions can be made.

Number 7 – After quietude an awakening to new realisations – the real world appears. Each hieroglyph shows the energy of missing contours, or the test, in its various guises. The 7-series shows the different reactions to an experience.

Number 8 – The moment to think about your choices. This is the moment of reflection about contradictions between your own possibilities and the forces of the world around you. The four hieroglyphs of the 8-series show the path to self-confidence and the four types of integration possible when a problem presents itself.

Number 9 – High mental and spiritual achievement. The moments that provoke you to look within, to discover your own truth. This energy pushes you to renew your endeavours, because both inner and outer realities become visible. Each hieroglyph of the 9-series shows us how your process expresses itself.

Number 10 – The manifestation that results out of all the preceding experiences. This energy includes both the seed of decay and unity after completing a cycle. The four hieroglyphs of the 10-series show how this energy expresses itself upon completion of a process.

Each set of guidance hieroglyphs is named as follows:

Rods = Ideas = The Path of Creative Ideas

Cups = Feelings = The Path of Love

Swords = Thought = The Path of Thought

Pentacles = Manifestation = The Path of Play

Section 2 – How to Use The Guidance Hieroglyphs

Here are a number of suggestions on how to work, or meditate with guidance hieroglyphs. These applications are not "set in stone." I recommend that you first gain some experience with the applications below and then begin experimenting with applications of your own. Some of these suggestions can also be applied to group work.

Seeking Guidance

If you are in a situation where you need help and are seeking guidance – for example, you do not know whether to accept a new position at your workplace – the following exercise can help you to facilitate your personal process.

1. Lay all 40 guidance hieroglyphs (the numbered cards of the Minor Arcana 1-10) face up. Select the one hieroglyph that attracts your attention.

2. Lay this chosen card in front of you as your first hieroglyph.

3. Pick a second hieroglyph with the intention that it represents your next step. Concentrate on the thought that this hieroglyph shows the outcome you would like in the future.

4. If you feel the need to choose more hieroglyphs to represent more steps then do so. Choose as many as you feel are necessary to help you in your personal process.

5. When you are done, read the interpretations in this book, bearing in mind that they serve as suggested meanings. Take some time to make your own interpretations of the guidance hieroglyphs, too.

6. Make notes of what you feel the hieroglyphs are telling you to do.

7. Put the hieroglyphs you have chosen in a special place. Work with your ideas for as long as you feel appropriate.

8. Return the hieroglyphs to your deck when you notice a change in your approach to the problem.

Breaking Repetitive Patterns

You may feel that you are repeatedly experiencing the same thing over and over again, either at work, home, or in relationships.

1. Before you pick your first guidance hieroglyph, read the interpretations of the cards.

2. After reading the interpretations, pick a hieroglyph that represents the catalyst for changing the pattern.

3. Lay it on a table, or on a special cloth. You may want to add pictures of people who you are experiencing the patterns with, add a talisman, or something you feel can protect you from repeating your

patterns.

4. Now look at the interpretations again with the intention of finding the guidance hieroglyphs that can help you to change your repetitive patterns. Choose as many as you feel are appropriate.

5. Lay these hieroglyphs alongside the first hieroglyph in the order you wish.

6. Keep the hieroglyphs in your mind's eye for a period of time.

7. When some time has passed, take all the hieroglyphs you have chosen to a tree or to a place in nature that is special to you and meditate with them there.

8. Return the hieroglyphs to your deck when you notice a change in your patterns.

Dealing With Grief Or Loss

This exercise will gradually allow your feelings to unfold naturally, help to strengthen you or help to balance you into a satisfactory equilibrium.

1. Look at the guidance hieroglyphs numbered 3, 5, 7, 8, 9 and 10.

2. Choose the hieroglyph that best represents your present feelings.

3. Use this hieroglyph as a channel to allow your feelings to surface and integrate the hieroglyph's energy into your thoughts.

4. Work and meditate with this hieroglyph for an appropriate period of time.

5. Make notes of the emotions you are experiencing. You may also want to take note of any dreams you remember while working with this hieroglyph.

6. If you wish, show your chosen hieroglyph to others close to you and discuss the experience that it depicts with them.

7. Return the hieroglyph to your deck when you notice a change in your process. Repeat this exercise if necessary.

Making Dreams Come True

You may be striving towards a "dream" career, saving for a "dream" holiday, or wanting to make a dream come true. This suggestion is designed to allow you to see the steps necessary to achieve the desired outcome.

1. Choose a guidance hieroglyph from the open deck that represents the empowerment you want to feel in order to make your "dream" come true.

2. Read the interpretation in this book and reflect on the hieroglyph. Draw, sing, or meditate with the hieroglyph in a special place.

3. Gain insights about its energy for a period of time.

4. Protect the hieroglyph you have picked with plastic, or wrap it in a special cloth, adding some lavender seeds, a rose quartz stone, and a strand of your hair. Leave this bundle in a special place, for example on an altar, for at least seven days.

5. In your mind, allow the energy of the hieroglyph to unfold itself. Open yourself to any outcome – including releasing or letting go of your "dream" – by practising meditation on a regular basis during this time.

6. Return the hieroglyph to your deck when you notice the energy has changed.

Making a Wish

Use this application if you wish to succeed in a project or want to support a relative or friend to succeed. It should only be used in a positive sense. This application can be used in groups.

1. Look at all the guidance hieroglyphs face up.

2. Choose the card that immediately attracts your attention.

3. Lay it on a table or on a one-coloured cloth.

4. Open your mind to any outcome – including releasing or letting go of the wish – by meditating, or writing a note that says that you accept any outcome.

5. Protect the hieroglyph you have picked with plastic, or wrap it in a special cloth, with some lavender seeds, a rose quartz stone, and a strand of your hair. Leave it in a special place for at least seven days.

6. Return the hieroglyph to your deck when you notice the energy has changed.

Releasing Blockages

It may be that contentment is missing or conflicts are weighing you down. Whatever – if you want to release or breakthrough blockages that disturb your natural flow in life, try the following layout. This application can also be used in group work.

1. Lay out your spiritual, personality, life, and lesson hieroglyph (add your hidden hieroglyph if you are a 19/10/(1) or have chosen one) on a one-coloured cloth.

2. Add the numbers on your personality, lesson, or hidden hieroglyph and reduce it to ten or under – remember the life hieroglyph is already a number under 10. (For example, if your personality hieroglyph is 18, add 1 + 8 = 9.)

3. Place the series of the guidance hieroglyphs you calculated (using above example this would be the 9-series) around your spiritual, personality, life, lesson, and hidden hieroglyph.

4. Read the interpretations of the cards and consider their meanings in your life.

5. Leave them in a special place for an appropriate period of time.

6. Use the time to develop your ability to release or break through your blockages with methods that suit your needs.

7. Return the hieroglyphs to your deck when you notice something has changed.

Conflicts in Intimate Relationships

You may require support during conflicts or problems in an intimate relationship. This exercise allows the hieroglyph's energy to unfold, since it means that you are opening the channel for change.

This exercise also functions as a reminder, enabling you and your partner to be more at ease about the knowledge in the "Path of Love", as laid out by ancient masters.

1. Take time to study the ten Path of Love (cups) guidance hieroglyphs with your partner. Discuss the energy that you perceive.

2. Talk to each other about the interpretations in this book and your own ideas. Aim at understanding and feeling what the path of these guidance hieroglyphs can teach you as a couple. Also aim to recognize in them the experience you as partners are presently going through.

3. Jointly make a resolution about how you are going to use these guidance hieroglyphs as channels of healing.

4. Choose a card that represents this resolution.

5. Lay the chosen hieroglyph in a special place for an appropriate period of time.

6. Jointly meditate or work with the hieroglyph in a way that suits both of your needs.

7. Return the hieroglyph to your deck when you notice a change in your situation, or in the energy around it.

Asking a Particular Question

I recommend that you **do not** consult the interpretations of the guidance hieroglyphs before trying this method. This application can be used in groups.

1. Lay all the guidance hieroglyphs face down on a special one-coloured cloth.

2. Write your question on a piece of paper and put it on the special cloth.

3. Choose as many hieroglyphs as you feel you may require to find the answer to your question.

4. The hieroglyphs you have chosen do not need to be kept in the order you chose them. Move them around as you wish.

5. Independently interpret the hieroglyphs and derive your answer to the question from your layout.

6. Return the hieroglyphs to your deck.

Section 3 – Interpretations of the Guidance Hieroglyphs

RODS – THE PATH OF CREATIVE IDEAS

Ace of Rods – *The Seed of Creativity*

You are at the beginning of an enterprise – creative energy allows movement to start. Your faculty of intuition is present in its entire simplicity. This is your chance to begin something by discovering and allowing nature to unfold. This is the moment when you know that problems can be removed. This energy can be compared to the natural fertility of nature.

2 of Rods – *Being in Command*

You sense how your willpower is at your disposal. It is time to give in to your unique inner power and to feel it at the present moment. You realise a project can be completed. At this moment, you balance between thought and desire. It is necessary to stick to action in order to reach completion. The hieroglyph shows you there is harmony when you are in command. It leads to justice in its purest form. You know a fire cannot burn without air, as otherwise it will smoulder.

3 of Rods – *Virtue*

This is the moment to use your willpower by infusing it with the necessary practical knowledge. A bit of time is needed, so you can successfully achieve a goal that includes the community. You have laid out a foundation; the initial success is seeded in a project or desire. You see the advantage of allowing it to express itself. You begin by affirming your path. This experience can be compared to the gardener who has sown a seed and runs to the garden to check whether it is sprouting. He then realises that things need time to grow.

4 of Rods – *Completion*

Now is the time to see something is enough – in the sense that 'enough' is exactly right. You have a sense of equilibrium because something has reached completion. You feel no inner agitation or restlessness. Somehow, you have found a way to control your natural impulses. To a certain extent you have become one with your environment. You have learnt that the moment you stand up to resistance it enables you to get an idea of what is available. You are like a farmer who has harvested the crops and modestly celebrates the occasion. There is a sense of inner growth inside. The fire you lit earlier is burning bright.

5 of Rods – *Endeavour*

An inner conflict comes to the surface. It causes you to feel aggressive and you wish you could use aggression to solve the problem. You notice you are dealing with contrary impulses, which cause you to think, "I must do the right thing at the right time". The situation you are confronted with seriously shakes you up. You feel challenged, but you step forward, taking a stance to the best of your ability in order to balance the situation. Symbolically seen, this situation is comparable to the moment when solid material begins to melt.

6 of Rods – *Victory*

You see how your endeavours are being rewarded. Gaining insights is part of this experience. Your victory means an inner transformation. You get a sense of inner harmony and see how this can be achieved without being inconsiderate. This hieroglyph's energy can also be identified as succeeding in transforming ideas. You feel you have gained self-confidence, trust, and belief, and inspire others with your knowledge.

7 of Rods – *Valour*

You notice the need to act with willpower, so that you stand in your power. It means you free yourself from formerly binding rules. You see that going into your inner darkness can help you overcome an inner block. This is the moment when you can let go of any fears and you get the power to overcome challenging situations with others. You add courage or bravery to your abilities in order to resolve problems. On an instinctive level, you see how life energy can be transformed and that giving in to opposing energy can allow you to stay in your power. This experience, figuratively speaking, is like the smell of the air after a thunderstorm on a humid summer day.

8 of Rods – *Swiftness*

This is the moment when a thought you never had before suddenly crosses your mind. You experience it as your possibility to make a quantum leap and correct past mistakes at the same time. You have the incentive to allow change to unfold. It seems as if what impeded your actions before cannot hold you back anymore. You see that acting quickly means that new energy is set free. Actions you took before are released and suddenly it makes you feel like a journey has come to an end.

9 of Rods – *Strength*

You allow your creative steps to become part of you. You see how you have learnt wisdom, and feel supported, or you gain creative power. You realise that you can rejuvenate. You feel mature and take initiative. Your creative-side shows when you can best influence a situation with what you have learnt. You set out to make your life blossom. In your soul, figuratively speaking, it is like the plants that grow pushing themselves through cement.

10 of Rods – *Yield*

You notice how you need to become more balanced. Something from either outside or inside seems to be slowing you down. This is your opportunity to view your next steps in their proper context. You see how important it is to gain ground. You say to yourself, "Seeds sprout in spring, but only if I allow winter to pass, as winter is part of it all". You conclude that this will allow the benefits of your experience to visibly show.

CUPS – THE PATH OF LOVE

Ace of Cups – *The Seed of Love*

The first spark of an emotion and your spirit feels like it is full, just waiting to spill out its emotions. This is the moment when the seed is filled with love; yet love doesn't disperse. You feel the hope of its fulfillment. It is like the beginning of a journey. You feel it as a birth of something that is completely new and pure. Symbolically it can be compared to the moment you unexpectedly discover something awesomely beautiful and you stop to watch its effect on you.

2 of Cups – *Love*

You give in to your feelings, because you wish to understand with your heart. You sense a balance in your heart and any action you pursue is connected to your sense of love. You express harmony, joy, and delight. You feel reborn and your body is filled with light, which gives you a sense of being connected to nature. You feel your soul is being purified by a new source that to you is an essential life force.

3 of Cups – *Abundance*

You feel as if a birth has taken place. Suddenly you are sucked into a vacuum and you cannot reverse its course. You have lost control over your emotions. Although your feelings get revived, you feel insecure; you sense what you are doing could backfire. However, you decide to see where uncontrolled feelings will take you. It is the moment when a dam has burst and the force of the water puts the environment at risk of damage.

4 of Cups – *Listening To Your Inner Voice*

You feel incapable of dealing with the present situation. You step back to review it. You attempt to separate yourself from its effect and take time to reflect on the mixed feelings you are experiencing. You take time to listen. At this moment happiness or sadness can surface, which makes you laugh or cry.

5 of Cups – *Disappointment*

Your feelings have suddenly disintegrated and loving emotions have dissolved. You sense a loss and see how you can help yourself by overcoming your inner resistance to it. You apply patience and live in the moment. You face your feelings, and it challenges and saddens you to see what feelings are within. These feelings are something you cannot move out of your way, but rather must face.

6 of Cups – *Joy*

You sense you have emotionally grown and you get a sense of inner reassurance. You feel an "inner switch" has opened you to development. You begin to see how situations in life do not stay the same and how feelings are like the changing cycles of nature. You realise that any past happiness can be brought into the present moment, if you are honest and sincere with yourself. You celebrate how your feelings can deepen your experience of love.

7 of Cups – *Disillusionment*

Your centre is out of balance, because your feelings have run dry. You see that success and order are illusory. You experience yourself as partly successful. You begin to re-examine your spiritual motives. You begin by striving to feel something resonate in your soul. Then you look at your goals and begin to allow yourself not to react or control what is plaguing you within.

8 of Cups – *Lethargy*

You feel a split between your feelings and mind. You lean back to feel their effect and it hurts to feel them. You realise that you must change your point of view. You decide to abandon striving for success by introducing modesty into your life. You face the fact of having put too much effort into things and begin by reflecting on your feelings. By exploring lethargy, later you are able to appreciate simple things more than before. Your spirit protects itself since it knows that this will cause lost energy to be regenerated. You find a place where you can retreat.

9 of Cups – *Blissfulness*

You realise that you can learn lessons from experiencing disappointments. This energy enables you to break through by dealing with feelings you have ignored in the past. These feelings are giving you a chance to reconcile yourself with the past. Reconciliation leads to bliss and bliss leads you to a clear intuitive awareness about the state of things. You feel you can walk on water without being at risk.

10 of Cups – *Saturation*

You experience the "sound" of love. You are like a mature plant developing seedpods. You see how your feelings have found a new expression. All your efforts are being rewarded. You are happy about your ability to develop further, because it makes you aware of your capabilities. You are reaping the benefits of allowing yourself to change. You have a sense of completion.

SWORDS – THE PATH OF THOUGHT

Ace of Swords – *The Seed Of Thought*

This is the moment when anything can happen as you naturally and willingly thrust yourself into allowing thoughts to unfold. Your imagination begins by connecting you to a fountain of knowledge, which seeds new thoughts. You allow thoughts to pass through your mind. You get a sense that there is an initial tension that makes you want to express your thoughts, but you first allow the flow of the thoughts to be birthed.

2 of Swords – *Peace*

You recognise the connection between your personal experience and what is in the world around you. You see opposites that make you feel ambivalent. Your mind begins to blend its masculine and feminine aspects in order to allow mind energy to flow. Applying wisdom when dealing with your willpower appears to stop the division you see. As a result, you decide that this will lead to peace. This is the moment you begin to serve a higher purpose for a good cause. Where there was once a demarcation line there is now a meeting point.

3 of Swords – *Grief*

You face sorrows and feel paralysed by them. The fact that opposites exist makes you feel sad. You feel like you are being pulled into an abyss full of thoughts, which weigh you down. You cannot resist its force or attempt to act as if everything was fine; you give in to your sorrows instead. This moment acts like a cleansing agent and you realise that all these feelings must surface.

4 of Swords – *Truce*

You realise that what has happened up to now has reached completion and you can stop thinking. You lose your attachment to certain values or qualities. Your mind gets clear and profound insights, where feelings have no place. You free yourself of suffering and relax. If you are faced with an attack, its result becomes secondary. Your reaction is not to act, as you know there is nothing to gain.

5 of Swords – *Defeat*

Your thoughts cause confusion within your spirit. You think you are put under pressure. Your mind realises that negative thoughts have triumphed. Your pride is broken. You experience this process as a mental overhaul and become willing to compromise, as it is the right time. Deep inside you stay confident and see how the choices you made have a good effect on your mind.

6 of Swords – *Integration*

Your mind rests by beginning to observe objective truths in your life. In order to overcome your inner resistance you allow unseen things to have their effect. Your mind reaches a more balanced approach so that danger may be evaded. You gain new knowledge while integrating former thoughts into your actions. You become stronger mentally.

7 of Swords – *Futility*

Your thoughts begin to cut through illusions that you didn't see before. You see something must be left behind and you must learn from lessons of the past. It causes you to see that your light within is weak and you feel pessimistic. Experiencing life's opportunities to learn anew makes you hang your head. You review your life by "heading out to a desert to howl with the wolves".

8 of Swords – *Interference*

The moment you see that energy is stuck. Something is holding you back. You are overcome by confusion, fears, and doubts. You try to overcome this situation by using the power of your mind. Facing this moment makes you fearful, you are unable to move.

9 of Swords – *Cruelty*

Your mind is dangerously persisting in negative thoughts. You have reached a dead end, as if a door has closed behind you. There is no way back and you see yourself as a helpless victim. Your mind resists change and is stuck in its negative thoughts, so that you decide to allow an element within you to pass.

10 of Swords – *Decline*

Your mind becomes plagued by insecurity and deep pain. You have absolutely no energy, so you become a victim of your destiny. You find this difficult to accept, but see no other option. You cease searching for solutions. Like a mourner at a funeral, your spirit is dressed in black. This moment can be compared to an electric circuit bursting with energy, but the electricity doesn't flow into the outlet.

PENTACLES – THE PATH OF PLAY

Ace of Pentacles – *The Seed Of Manifestation*

You see the purity of material things while facing ordinary reality in its simplest form. You open yourself to this energy completely. You feel it as an eternal synthesis, which you can counterbalance if necessary. You enjoy and welcome this moment as if it were a gift spreading itself out in front of you.

2 of Pentacles – *Change*

You allow manifestation to flow in harmony with the vibrations of life, which enables you to welcome change. You naturally swing between the vibrations you sense. You send a new message to others around you, as your body is permitting change to become part of you. You go with the flow, feeling synchronised.

3 of Pentacles – *Work*

You work on creating results by bringing the physical and spiritual search within you into balance. You concentrate on smaller details with a constructive plan in mind. With the assistance of others, you feel satisfied and help complete the plan. You sense yourself gaining ground through cooperation with others.

4 of Pentacles – *Stability*

Your feelings are stimulated by an earthly power. You see that something can be won from observing manifestation under the light of day. It is time to understand fears in order to overcome fears within you. It makes you stable and you can gather new energy. You learn to respect new ideas as they evolve.

5 of Pentacles – *Torment*

You retreat from action, as your work has been destroyed. Nothing fits, so you experience it as dispersal. You are overcome by worries because you have lost something. You see you can gain something from breaking your attachment to material things, but almost feel tortured by not knowing what to do.

6 of Pentacles – *Balance*

You have been brought back to a more sober approach. You have a clear perception of your situation. You slowly restore your confidence and see how the progress of your efforts is bearing fruit. You are on the right course and life seems to be on your side. You sense that success is on the horizon.

7 of Pentacles – *Challenge*

You realise that you have done the correct thing but put your effort into the wrong project. You pause to check what has developed from this. You consider alternative approaches and try to find out where you stand in order to get a sense of the direction you could take. Any fears arising allow you to look seriously at your past mistakes.

8 of Pentacles – *Cleverness*

You prudently establish your mission. You become aware of things you didn't know before and start to understand them more deeply. You collect information that anchors your goals.

9 of Pentacles – *Gain*

You begin seeing results arising from your work. You are complacent and notice within your spirit that you have quietly shifted gears. You realise your foresight is showing in your work. You feel uplifted and gain confidence to persevere. You think you have found the correct degree of effort necessary.

10 of Pentacles – *Wealth*

You transcend to reach completion. You can clearly see the gains and losses of your efforts. You look at your work while feeling connected to another source that grounds you in a different way. You have contributed to enriching your environment. Before, you felt as if you were floating above the ground; now your experience is that you are in touch with the earth.

Summary

This topic is extensive and this guidebook is an introduction. I very much hope that the Inner Flame method becomes a method that you enjoy integrating into your daily life. Please know that I am available to support you in your endeavours. Apart from giving lectures and offering workshops on this subject I am also available for counseling and questions on my website >www.innerflame.net<.

SUGGESTED READING

Anderson, Mary, *Numerology, The Secret Power of Numbers,* Aquarian Press, Wellingborough, First Edition, 1972.

Arrien, Angeles, *The Tarot Handbook*, Aquarian, London, 1991,©1987.

Bailey, E.H., *Astrology & the Cards*, Foulsham & Co., London, [1930].

Banzhaf, Hajo, *Das Tarot Handbuch*, Hugendubel, Munich, 1986.

Bohnenkamp, Axel, *Tarot als Lebenshilfe*, Goldmann, Munich , 1986.

Bumstead, George, *Occult Works*, Brandon, London, 1852.

Case, Paul Foster, The Tarot, *A Key to the Wisdom of the Ages* (with illustrations), Macoy Publishing Co., New York, 1947.

Cayce, Edgar, *The Hidden Laws of Earth*, by Juliet Brooke Ballard, Virginia Beach, Virginia, 1979.

Cayce, Edgar, *Ueber Sexualitaet und Erleuchtung*, Goldmann, 1989.

Cheasley, Clifford, W., *Numerology, It's Practical Applications to Life*, Revised, Rider & Son, London, 1923.

Drach, David, *The Quabalah, The Tradition of the West by Papus* (Gérard Encausse), 2nd edition, Thorsons, Wellingborough, 1977.

Gray, Eden, *The Tarot Revealed*, (5th printing), New York American Library, 1969.

Fortune, Dion, *The Mystical Qabalah*, E.Benn, London, 1958, 1957, 1970.

Golowin, Sergius, *Die Welt des Tarot*, Sphinx Verlag, Basel, 1976.

Greer, Mary, *Tarot for Yourself*, Aquarian, Wellingborough, c1984.

Hoeller, Stephan, A., *The Royal Road, A Manual of Kabalistic Meditations on the Tarot,* Theosophical Publishing House, Wheaton, III.. London 1975.

Kerenyi, Karl, *The Heroes of the Greeks*, Thames & Hudson, London, ©1959, 1997 printing.

Leuenberger, Hans-Dieter, *Schule des Tarot*, Bauer, Freiburg i. Br., 1981.

Levi, Eliphas, *The Book of Splendours*, Aquarian, Wellingborough, 1972.

Lionel, Frederic, *L'Enigme Que Nous Sommes, The Seduction of the Occult Path,* translation by Robin Campbell, Turnstone, Wellingborough, 1983.

Lionel, Frederic, *Presence de la Grande Tradition, Ses Symbole et Ses Nombres*, Editions Robert Lafont, Paris, 1975.

Lionel, Frederic, *The Magic Tarot*, translation M.W. Gadzuk, Routledge & Kagan, Paul, London 1982.

Metzner, Rolf, *Maps of Consciousness*, Collier Books, New York, London, 1974.

Metzner, Ralph, *The Well of Remembrance*, Shambhala, Boston, Massachusetts, London, 1994.

Montano, Mario, *Tarot – Spiegel des Lebens*, Urania-Verlag, Sauerlach, 1988.

Nordic, Rolland, K., *The Tarot Shows the Path*, Regency Press, London, 1960.

Papus, pseud.[i..e. Gérald Encausse] translated by A. Morton, *Absolute Key to Occult Science, The Tarot of the Bohemians, The most ancient book in the world...,* (translated by A.P. Morton) 2nd edition revised, Chapman + Hall, London, 1892.

Peach, Emily, *The Tarot for Tomorrow*, Aquarian, Wellingborough, 1988.

Peach Emily, *Das Tarot-Werkbuch*, Scherz, Vienna, Bern, Munich, 1987.

Pollack, Rachel, *Tarot – The Open Labyrinth*, Aquarian, Wellingborough, 1986.

Raman, Dio, *Der Praktische Tarot*, Bauer Verlag, Freiburg i. Br., 1981.

Rosendaal, H., *Hermetic Magick*, New Order Publications, Aberdeen, 1973.

Slinger, Penny and Nik, Douglas, *Das Grosse Buch des Tantra,* Sphinx Verlag, Basel, 1985.

Stoll, Johann Gottlieb, *Etwas Zur Richtigen Beurteilung der Theosophie, Cabbala, Magie und Anderer Geheimer Uebernatuerliche Wissenschaften, etc.*, Leipzig, 1786.

Thorsson, Edred, *Handbuch der Runen-Magie*, Urania-Verlag, Sauerlach, 1987.

Usscher, Arland, *The Twenty-Two Keys of the Tarot*, new edition, Dolmen Press, Dublin, 1976.

Uxkull, Woldemar, *Die Einweihung im Alten Aegypten*, Argenbuehl-Egolfstal, 1981.

Vanstone, John Henry, *The Pathway of the Soul*, "Modern Astrology", London, 1912.

EXAMPLE OF LIFE LESSON DIAGRAM

for birth date 8 April 1962, looking at past lessons (1962–1970) and future lessons (2004–2006):

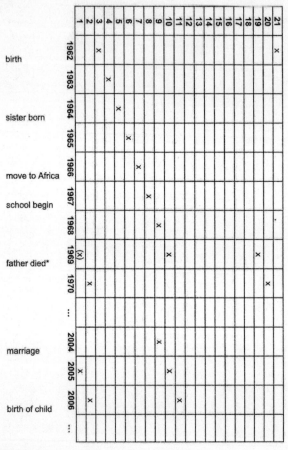

* i.e. for 1969, the year that father died:

      8 (day of birth)

+   4 (month of birth)

+ <u>1969</u> (year father died)

    1981   thus 1+9+8+1=19, 1+9=10, 1+0=1

Three lesson cards, including one hidden for that year: 19/10/(1)

the FINDHORN book of . . .

Building Trust in Groups
David Earl Platts, PhD
isbn 1-84409-017-5

Guidance & Intuition
Carly Newfeld
isbn 1-84409-008-6

Vegetarian Recipes
Kay Lynne Sherman
isbn 1-84409-015-9

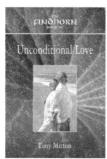

Unconditional Love
Tony Mitton
isbn 1-84409-006-X

Connecting with Nature
John R Stowe
isbn 1-84409-011-6

Forgiveness
Michael Dawson
isbn 1-84409-012-4

Meditation
Darren John Main
isbn 1-84409-005-1

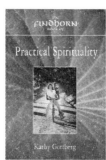

Practical Spirituality
Kathy Gottberg
isbn 1-84409-007-8

*and many more
to come...*

FINDHORN
Press

Findhorn Press is a publishing business of the
Findhorn Community which has grown around the
Findhorn Foundation in northern Scotland.

For further information about the Findhorn Foundation and the
Findhorn Community please contact:

Findhorn Foundation
The Visitors Centre
The Park, Findhorn IV36 3TZ, Scotland, UK
tel 01309 690311 • fax 01309 690301
email vcentre@findhorn.org
www.findhorn.org

For a complete Findhorn Press catalogue, please contact:

Findhorn Press
305a The Park, Findhorn
Forres IV36 3TE, Scotland, UK
Tel 01309 690582, freephone 0800-389-9395
Fax 01309 690036

if you live in the USA or Canada, please send your request to:

Findhorn Press
c/o Lantern Books
One Union Square West, Suite 201
New York, NY 10003-3303

Wherever you live, you can consult our catalogue online at
www.findhornpress.com
and email us at info@findhornpress.com